Share the Wealth

Share the Wealth

How to End Rentier Capitalism

Philippe Askenazy

Translated by Gregory Elliott

V

VERSO

London • New York

This English-language edition first published by Verso 2021
First published as *Tous rentiers!: Pour une autre répartition des richesses*
© Odile Jacob 2016
Translation © Gregory Elliott 2021

1 3 5 7 9 10 8 6 4 2

Verso
UK: 6 Meard Street, London W1F 0EG
US: 20 Jay Street, Suite 1010, Brooklyn, NY 11201
versobooks.com

Verso is the imprint of New Left Books

ISBN-13: 978-1-78873-937-5
ISBN-13: 978-1-78873-939-9 (US EBK)
ISBN-13: 978-1-78873-938-2 (UK EBK)

British Library Cataloguing in Publication Data
A catalogue record for this book is available from the British Library

Library of Congress Cataloging-in-Publication Data
A catalog record for this book is available from the Library of Congress
Library of Congress Control Number: 2020947559

Typeset in Minion Pro by MJ & N Gavan, Truro, Cornwall
Printed in the UK by CPI Group (UK) Ltd, Croydon, CR0 4YY

Contents

Acknowledgements

This essay was inspired by constant discussion with Katia. I must thank Odile Jacob, who knew exactly how to motivate me, as well as her team, particularly Gaëlle Jullien, for their support and careful attention in reading the French manuscript. The Verso team and Gregory Elliott supplied their decisive expertise to adapt the text for an international audience. This updated and expanded version of *Tous rentiers!* (Paris: Odile Jacob, 2016) has also benefited from comments following presentations, especially at the International Labour Organization in Geneva, UCLouvain and the University of Luxembourg.

Introduction

Whereas universal and lasting peace can be established only if it is based upon social justice;

And whereas conditions of labour exist involving such injustice, hardship and privation to large numbers of people as to produce unrest so great that the peace and harmony of the world are imperilled; and an improvement of those conditions is urgently required ...

Preamble to the Constitution of the International Labour Organization (ILO), adopted in Philadelphia, 10 May 1944, reiterating the initial considerations of chapter 13, creating the ILO, from the Versailles Peace Treaty, signed on 28 June 1919

In the United States, the Democrats are struggling to prevent the re-election of Donald Trump. Across the Atlantic, European social democracy has collapsed. It holds barely 20 per cent of the seats in the European Parliament elected in May 2019. For the most part, its historical parties of government[1] have been reduced to the role of junior partner in a coalition, like the SPD in Germany,

---

1   At an international level, they are grouped under the banner of the Progressive Alliance, which also includes the US and Korean Democratic parties.

when they have not virtually disappeared, like the French Social-
ists or Greece's PASOK. For now, ecologists or anti-capitalists have
only filled the political vacuum on an occasional basis. Despite
the tumult of Brexit, Labour was not able to return to office. It
took the exceptional combination of a major institutional crisis
with Catalonia and a widespread corruption scandal for a socialist
without a majority to come to power in Spain. In East Asia, too,
only a major scandal in 2017 installed a democrat in the South
Korean presidency. In Japan, since the start of the century, democrats and social democrats have only been in power for a brief
interlude of three years.

The Left Caught in the Trap of the Neoliberal Fable

Yet, well before the Covid-19 crisis, awareness of climate change,
denunciation of madcap finance, and civic movements of the '99
per cent' should have resulted in domination by social democracy,
as well as a modern US liberalism, and potentially led to a renewal of
the trade unions close to these currents. But their ideas and actions
have remained imprisoned in the straitjacket of the fables of neoliberalism. One of these concerns the origins of inequalities in the
advanced economies: primary inequalities – prior to redistribution
– are said to be natural and reflect people's individual productivity. The disturbing increase in them over recent decades allegedly
derives from globalization and, even more so, the technological
revolutions that inexorably polarize society between winners and
losers. On the winners' side are capitalists, the heroes of the entre-
preneurial class, professional experts, senior management, and so
forth. On the losers' side are routinized workers, the unproductive,
the toiling classes, who are set to disappear or experience stagnation in their incomes. Spatial inequalities themselves supposedly
mirror productivity differentials between regions. This trend, dictated by technology, is bound to continue. With the gig economy,[1]

---

1   There is no agreed definition of 'gig', which is short for 'engagement'.
We may, for example, use the following: 'a gig describes a single project or task

the employed wage-earning class has entered its twilight years. With robots and artificial intelligence, the jobs of the so-called middle class, already in decline, will disappear.

Subscribing to this fable involves an insidious defeatism – a defeatism that may be characterized as 'progressive neoliberalism', to adopt a term used by the feminist philosopher Nancy Fraser in analysing the defeat of Hillary Clinton.[1]

'Progressivists' call for secondary redistribution to bring about a more egalitarian allocation of wealth and ensure the development of the whole of a territory. But this strategy is no longer feasible. How can consent to taxation be maintained when growing primary inequality requires more corrective social transfers at the expense of investments in the public services, including hospitals? How can investment and redistribution via taxation be promoted in societies a majority of whose members are small property owners, who reject taxation on assets other than, perhaps, those of the very wealthy?

Hence the conversion to a third way that has its origins in Blairism and Clinton's period of governance. In the name of pragmatism and efficiency, the goal of equality is abandoned in favour of an illusory equality of opportunity. Universal education remains a priority, but beyond that everyone will get a minimal welfare safety net, to enable them to bounce back. Spatial mobility must help people to leave behind an area condemned to decline. Thus will everyone be the entrepreneur of their own life, which will have the effect of blurring social origins. Protected work contracts are accused of obstructing equality of opportunity by erecting barriers to employment for the unemployed and casual workers. Privatization makes it possible not only to boost public finances, but also to abolish such barriers.

---

for which a worker is hired, often through a digital marketplace, to work on demand'. Elka Topey and Andrew Hogan, 'Working in the Gig Economy', *BLS Career Outlook* (May 2016).

1   Nancy Fraser, 'The End of Progressive Neoliberalism', *Dissent* (January 2017).

Thus, equality of opportunity is not content to take cognizance of a neoliberal order; it consolidates it. In the advanced economies, 'considered' reforms must abolish 'dogmas' – read: reduce workers' protections and rights where they still exist – in order to adapt society to the neoliberal order. If they are not to hamper competitiveness, workers' demands must be 'reasonable'. Such was the agenda of Matteo Renzi in Italy and of François Hollande in France in the mid 2010s – the latter accentuated by Emmanuel Macron.

However, abandoning the goal of equality leaves the biggest barriers to social mobility intact: social and geographical origin, parental financial resources, leisure activities, schools attended – these are powerful determinants in defining people's career opportunities, and even their health.

And support for the neoliberal order undermines a key facet of the progressive programme: the struggle against the economic discrimination suffered by women and various minorities. For the latter are overrepresented among the *unproductive* who, *naturally*, must be poorly remunerated for their work.

How are we to escape these impasses? What must be done for social democracy once again to become a credible alternative to neoliberalism? How can it be helped to reformulate its own theoretical infrastructure?

Inequalities Accrue from an Allocation of Rents

To break with a pragmatism that has proved deadly, we must dare to delve into the contemporary capitalist order. An initial step, which this book proposes to take, consists in overturning the ideas that have trapped social democracy and liberalism. Basically, primary distribution is not natural: it results from an allocation of rents. To demonstrate this, we need to deconstruct the formation of 'rents' and the capacity of each social group to capture them.

The term 'rents' will be used throughout this work. I shall employ a broad definition: rents are advantages that can be extracted on an ongoing basis by certain economic actors (capitalists, financiers, property owners, wage-earners, the self-employed, entrepreneurs, states, and so on) via economic, political or legal mechanisms potentially open to influence by them. They can take the form of monetary income, but also of non-pecuniary things such as living conditions, including working conditions and social recognition. This definition endeavours to encompass various approaches to rents.

Legal science and accountancy have their own formal definitions of rent or rents. In economics, the term has a wide range of meanings. The major classical authors of the eighteenth and nineteenth centuries, from David Ricardo to Karl Marx, introduced ground rent alongside capitalist (surplus-)profit and wages. Landowners receive a rent in return for use of their land. In Ricardo, this 'differential' rent benefits those who own the best land, as the prices of agricultural products are fixed in relation to production costs on the least fertile land. Marx adds to it absolute rent, also called monopoly rent: even the owners of less fertile land have incomes derived from the monopoly on this land conferred by ownership.

Economists of different schools of thought next extended the notion of monopoly rent to all economic activities where an economic actor wields market power and can extricate herself from competition to impose unfair prices on customers. With the extension of the domain of property, rents become associated with the possession of intangible assets – patents, databases, and so forth. In other fields, reference is made to the 'situational rent' of someone who enjoys a privilege, a form of protection, or an advantageous location for their business.

Today, 'rent' is widely used in economics to characterize situations where an economic actor obtains an advantage at the expense of another actor. The term often implies a judgement. Consequently, the precise terminology varies depending on the author's view or ideological position. Thus, in wage negotiations between a trade union and an employer, some will speak of 'workers' rent', meaning concessions extracted from the employer by the union, others of 'employer's rent', meaning the concessions made by employees faced with the threat of layoffs. In the US political context, Joseph Stiglitz defines 'rent seeking' as 'many of the ways by which our current political process helps the rich at the expense of the rest of us'.[1]

As we shall see in the first part of this book, technological, ideological and geopolitical shocks can create new sources of rents, and call into question both the size of current rents and their continuation and allocation. Thus, an industrial revolution destroys rents based on old technologies, but also opens up new opportunities. The extension of the market economy – the transition of the former Soviet bloc, or the commodification of health – also rejigs the economic game. Actors with a strong hand appropriate a growing share of wealth.

An account of the evolution of rents and their sources in recent decades,[2] followed by an unpacking of the mechanics of their appropriation, reveals the super-armament of a capitalism now freed from the communist threat. 'Propertarianism' is the decisive lever:[3] 'all is property' goes far beyond the advantages of landownership and extends to property rights in intangibles: databases, patents, and so on. Along with privatization (including of public services), propertarianism enables capitalists to amass sizeable rents.

On the side of labour, the profound changes affecting individuals and the content of their jobs facilitate new forms of domination:

---

1   Joseph Stiglitz, *The Price of Inequality: How Today's Divided Society Endangers Our Future* (New York: W.W. Norton, 2013), p. 48.

2   By contrast, I will not partake in a statistical approach extending over a century or more. In the first instance, this is in order to root my argument more firmly in the present. Secondly, as we shall see throughout this work, the available data do not make it possible to conduct such an exercise reliably or without potential anachronisms.

3   Thomas Piketty provides his own approach to propertarianism in his last book *Capital and Ideology* (Cambridge, MA: Harvard University Press, 2020). It partially overlaps with but differs from my analysis that I introduced in the first French version of this book, published in 2016.

posts deemed 'unproductive' are in fact subject to work intensification, become rich in skills, and generate productivity increases that feed capitalistic rents. These increases are concealed, even denied, by statistical tools ill-adapted to understanding contemporary work. As for the worker who is an independent entrepreneur, she is a myth when relations of subordination of employees to their employer persist or are even reinforced.

Yet the world of work also has its winners: certain corporations elude the imperative of competitiveness and derive situational rents that bear no relation to their effort. Sometimes, they even succeed in focusing the attention and safety expenditure of enterprises on their working conditions when they have not deteriorated.

The major arguments naturalizing the distribution of income and wages are therefore partial in both senses of the word. The allocation of wealth and effort proves malleable.

The second part of this book examines the prospects for renewed social progress. How are we to get to the root of things and refashion the primary distribution of rents? This book proposes some paths. On the one hand, it involves rehabilitating labour and recognizing the efforts of those who find themselves characterized as unproductive. To this end, we cannot make do simply with minimum wages or universal income. Paying tribute and applauding the 'essential' workers during the pandemic lockdown will not likely shake the social order, and the terrible recession in 2020 may even strengthen it. Above and beyond that, the world of work must be remobilized. It is not only essential during exceptional circumstances, but it is *critical* for the regular operation of businesses and public services. Contrary to a widespread belief, it is neither amorphous nor shattered nor mortally threatened by technology. From the United States to Europe, modes of mobilization have emerged that, while certainly embryonic, are innovative. As we shall see, they could be extended. On the other hand, it is a question of weakening capital by destabilizing propertarianism in both respects: 'everyone a property owner' and 'all is property'.

A final thought before proceeding to the substance of the matter: redefining the primary allocation of wealth is not simply a matter of social justice, public health or economic dynamics. In scorning labour's contribution to wealth-creation, in stigmatizing those who deliver growth as unproductive, neoliberal capitalism fuels profound anger, even in countries said to have full employment.

The French philosopher Grégoire Chamayou describes the emergence from the 1970s onwards of an 'authoritarian liberalism' characterized by a strong state.[1] It arrived in response to a 'crisis of governability' created by a kind of excess of democracy in which social and environmental protests against the capitalist order were intertwined. Today, protest has given way to a 'great unrest' (to use the words of the ILO Constitution). Three decades after the fall of the Berlin Wall, neoliberal capitalism seems sustainable only through a deflection of resentment onto sections of the population – in the first instance, immigrants – in increasingly authoritarian regimes. From this perspective, the war against the Covid-19 pandemic offers additional opportunities to strengthen the social control of the population.

From European social democrats via British Labourists to US liberals, all have a responsibility to renew themselves to avoid such confrontations – or, worse, a combination of neoliberalism, anti-immigrant populism and authoritarianism. All the more so because such a drift precludes thought and progress on the great issues of the twenty-first century.

Disclaimer

The manuscript of this book was completed in August 2019. I made the choice not to delay its publication by integrating material on the Covid-19 pandemic, except briefly in the introduction.

---

1   See Grégoire Chamayou, *La Société ingouvernable* (Paris: La Fabrique, 2018).

On the one hand, it would have been necessary to wait many months to have the necessary hindsight on the events. On the other, for the time being, I interpret the health, social, democratic and economic crisis that is hitting many countries as a dramatic illustration not of a capitalism sick with the coronavirus but of a capitalism sick with itself. It is precisely because it sheds light on this underlying morbidity that this book could help us to think of a 'world after'.

1

Fascination with the 1 Per Cent

In the closing years of the twentieth century, capitalism became faceless. Worker and consumer alike found themselves confronting elusive but domineering spectres: those of finance and the multinationals, from vulture funds to Monsanto. Capitalists had disappeared behind acronyms. And the heads of small or medium-sized enterprises were reduced to the status of subcontractors exploited by these powers.

The only capitalists still possessing a face, from the American Bill Gates (Microsoft) via the Italian Sergio Marchionne (Ferrari) or the Korean Lee family (Samsung) to the French Pinault dynasty (Gucci), were characterized as brilliant entrepreneurs or inventors; their success was construed exclusively as the consecration of their qualities. Furthermore, these men (rarely women) were patrons of prominent cultural and social causes. Wealth was not taboo because it was an engine for the most innovative, and would trickle down to the rest of society.

The 1 Per Cent as the New Face of Capitalism

Little by little, a change occurred at the start of the twenty-first century. Capitalism once again had a face: the wealthiest, the '1 per cent', even the super-rich – the billionaires who feature on the *Forbes* list. Materially replete, the only thing most of these wealthy rentiers lacked was notoriety. Accordingly, some of them did all they could to emerge from obscurity. Thus, we discovered Paris Hilton, the immensely rich inheritor of the Hilton hotel chain. After starting out as a mannequin in charity parades, she burst onto the media scene by co-hosting a US reality TV show. A veritable popular phenomenon, she fuels magazines (female and male!), where we learn that her feet are size eleven. Meanwhile, the public experiences a mixture of fascination and discomfort with these idle lives where jet-setters, toy boys and toy girls bump into one another. A whole bestiary populates a parallel universe.

The ambivalent feelings aroused by this universe are even conveyed by children's games. In the brilliant introduction to the book he has devoted to the rich,[1] Thierry Pech unpacks the mutation of Monopoly. In twentieth-century Monopoly, the wealthy man lived what on the whole was an 'ordinary' life: he paid hospital charges, bought a house, and even paid taxes on his properties. In today's Monopoly, he buys an island or a whole town, celebrates his birthday on a privatized Australian beach, or receives a tax rebate of 500,000 euros, pounds or dollars.

And then, whether it is the spectacle of the Bettencourt family (L'Oréal) in France, the nepotism of the Korean chaebols, or the multiple tax-avoidance schemes that cater to American fortunes, the wealthy end up becoming tiresome and shocking.

Meanwhile, academic works on the wealthy proliferate and circulate widely. For example, in France the works of the sociologist couple Monique and Michel Pinçon-Charlot, such as *Ghettos du Gotha*, have met with great success. In this context, a group of economists has put some figures on this particular face of capital. Sir Anthony Atkinson, British pioneer of studies of inequality, has been joined by two French figures, Emmanuel Saez and Thomas

---

1   Thierry Pech, *Le Temps des riches. Anatomie d'une sécession* (Paris: Seuil, 2011).

Piketty.[1] Using fiscal sources, they have constructed a very broad longitudinal body of data over the long term, describing the share of total national income taken by the highest incomes. Their data reveal the capture of an increasing share of national income by a very small minority: not the wealthiest 10 per cent, but essentially the 1 per cent. This phenomenon is global, but is more marked in the Anglophone countries – especially the United States, where the share of the 1 per cent returned in the 2010s to its level at the start of the twentieth century, when it received more than 20 per cent of national income, as against 15 per cent in the UK and a little less than 10 per cent in France and Japan.

The value of large estates has also grown much more rapidly than global GDP. Moreover, the higher one goes – reaching one-thousandth of the wealthiest and then one-millionth – the more income and wealth have advanced. Income and wealth are in fact closely linked, a significant portion of income now being derived from wealth, not from work.

These analyses of the 1 per cent, as well as those by Joseph Stiglitz, directly inspired the slogan of Occupy Wall Street: 'We are the 99 per cent.' European movements of *indignados* – while more influenced by *Indignez-vous!*, by another Frenchman, Stéphane Hessel – have also deployed the spectre of the 1 per cent in their arguments.

The enormous global success in 2014 of Thomas Piketty's book, *Capital in the Twenty-First Century*,[2] tended to confirm a switch from fascination to denunciation. Among radicals and

1   The work of Piketty and Saez has earned them the highest rewards for young economists in Europe and the United States, respectively. Saez is professor at the University of California, and Piketty at the École des Hautes Etudes en Sciences Sociales in Paris. Their bi-continental reach helps to diffuse their findings widely. Above all, it enables them to construct a core body of data on key territories – the United States and European countries – and to bring together a sizeable team to perform this exercise on numerous countries. (The data can be freely accessed on wid.world.)

2   Thomas Piketty, *Capital in the Twenty-First Century*, transl. Arthur Goldhammer (Cambridge: Harvard University Press, 2014).

a number of American liberals, it held out hope for a wake-up call that might lead to a tax revolution. However, less than three years later, Donald Trump, a billionaire – epitomizing the images of the self-made man and the reality TV star to be found among the 1 per cent – was installed in the White House, implementing a programme at the antipodes of Piketty's prescriptions. How are we to interpret such a disappointment?

The Theory of the 1 Per Cent Exploited by the 0.1 Per Cent

The resonance of Piketty's book in 2014, in the United States and then elsewhere, was a cause of much surprise in France. On its appearance in French in 2013, it met with only moderate success in the bookshops. In the United States, Occupy Wall Street was already in its third year of existence when the book came out. Above all, it is a thick academic tome. To understand the enthusiasm it generated, we must return to the various stages of the launch of the US edition. We shall see that the relevance of this far exceeds the secrets of creating a bestseller; we are dealing, rather, with the construction of the dominant economic and political ideas.

It was Paul Krugman, winner of the Bank of Sweden prize in memory of Alfred Nobel and one of the most widely read commentators in the United States, who fired the opening salvos upon the release of the English-language version. In his column, he proclaimed that the book furnished irrefutable proof of the excesses of US capitalism and the appetites of the wealthiest. This column was to trigger a coordinated riposte, frequently in bad faith – even violent – from (neo)conservative circles. This prompted, in turn, a counter-offensive from radical intellectuals and the media. Since the book was not distributed by a mass-market publisher, buyers had to go via the internet in very large numbers to purchase it. It thus became a bestseller on Amazon.com – which accelerated its sales, and hence the media loop. The same scenario of frontal assaults and counter-offensives was repeated upon its publication in Britain. The *Financial Times*, the pre-eminent organ of the world of finance, even claimed on its front page to have detected manipulation of the data. In every country where the book was translated, it was the same story.

The seeming naivety of neoliberals and neoconservatives is astounding. By attacking the book so heavily, and the author sometimes so directly, they ensured its promotion, and thereby maximized the audience for the ideas it was defending. How could the same conservatives who for decades had proved adept at manipulating opinion in the economic and geopolitical arenas alike have made such a mistake?

A return to France suggests a different interpretation. The Hexagon has its own share of neoliberals (and even neocons). Private discussions with some of them evinced no particular hostility towards the identification of the 1 per cent as the central sign of inequality. On the contrary, they seemed comfortable enough with it. In fact, that a book which was social-democratic in inspiration should become central, and that its author could be characterized as the new Karl Marx, was experienced as a lesser evil compared with the risk of radical, even revolutionary, movements in the context of the Socialist Party's anticipated meltdown. Similarly, it is very reassuring to have a Pope Francis resurrecting within the Church (which maintains its reactionary social teachings) the ecological question and the condemnation of Mammon long consigned to 'leftists'.

How is it that most analyses of the 1 per cent are not unduly dangerous for capital? In short, they are not conducive to challenging capitalism itself, whether in a Marxist idiom – 'alienation of the workers' – or for its environmental ravages. They displace contestation of capitalism onto the rich and their apparent egotism. Better still (and doubtless this is the key point) they take for granted, or confirm, the natural character of the primary allocation of income – that is, income distribution prior to taxation and redistribution between workers and between capital and labour. Let us consider two arguments that structure current debates.

The most-cited works on the stratospheric and significantly increasing incomes of senior executives are those of Xavier Gabaix and Augustin Landier.[1] They rationalize the distribution of CEOs' incomes, presented as proportional to the sizes of their enterprises. Hierarchy framed as meritocratic, with the 'best' at the head of the largest firms. According to their estimations, placing at the head of the 250th enterprise the CEO of the first would guarantee it a higher profit (of the order of 10 per cent). Although this gradient is very shallow, the sums at stake for shareholders are such that it is *natural* for them to pay salaries to attract the best. However, this argument is decidedly weak. In fact, even if we accept their results, the authors ignore the effects of pronounced social reproduction, in which the personnel involved are drawn from the same caste of graduates from a few elite universities. The hierarchy they observe exists only within the tiny class of the CEOs in post. And nothing proves that the manager "n-4" of the same enterprises would not obtain better results if they were made CEOs.

The Meaning of Equations

The 'first basic law of capitalism' formulated by Thomas Piketty derives from the same logic of naturalization. This 'law' is above all a computable, hence exact, equation: the share of the income of capital α is equal to the product of the average rate of return of capital r and the capital/income relationship, denoted as β: $\alpha = r \times \beta$.

Marxist theory writes the same computable equation differently: $r = \alpha/\beta$.

Seemingly minor, this difference is in fact major. In the Marxist interpretation in *Capital*, the share α is the translation of capital's

---

1   French economists based in the United States at the time of their initial texts. In 2014 they published an updated version of their work on this theme. See Xavier Gabaix, Augustin Landier and Julien Sauvagnat, 'CEO Pay and Firm Size: An Update after the Crisis', *Economic Journal* 124 (2014), pp. F40–F59.

capacity to appropriate rents. The return r can be constant, because β increases when α grows. In effect, β is not a physical measure of capital, but the monetary value of assets that grows a priori when investments yield greater profits. Taken to an extreme, this reading embodies the communist idea of socialization of the means of production. In the context of a market economy, it identifies levers for a fairer society: labour movements, class struggle, or the social and cooperative economy.

In *Capital in the Twenty-First Century*, the return on capital r is regarded as largely given: it is the translation of *natural* technological parameters, like the marginal productivity of capital and the replacement of labour by capital. Furthermore, according to Piketty, this return is relatively constant over the long term. The weight of profit α is thus the simple outcome of the accumulation of capital.

In this framework, primary inequalities can decrease only when the rate of economic growth exceeds the return on capital – something observed in the major countries of the Organisation for Economic Cooperation and Development (OECD) only during the decades following the Second World War.

Given natural primary inequalities, and faced with weak or moderate growth, the reduction of inequality has to be conceived at a secondary level – that is, it must essentially take the form of redistribution, in the form of a highly progressive tax system of the 'Robin Hood' variety. This is the core of Piketty's book, which for example evokes a hypothetical global tax on large estates. It is also that of Atkinson,[1] who proposed operational strategies for the pre-Brexit UK. This guiding principle has long been found in the programmes of the main European social-democratic parties as well as the US Democratic Party.

---

1   Anthony B. Atkinson, *Inequality: What Can Be Done?* (Cambridge: Harvard University Press, 2015). Atkinson also proposes increasing the minimum wage in the UK and creating an economic and social council to encourage social dialogue.

Redistribution at an Impasse

Yet this efflorescence of works hardly perturbs capital, neoliberals and neoconservatives. On both sides of the Atlantic, analyses – for example, by the US economist Richard Freeman and the French sociologists Michel Pinçon and Monique Pinçon-Charlot – say the same thing. On the one hand, the way US politics is financed ensures a pragmatic majority within the Democratic Party; on the other, 'the series of renunciations must be situated within the long history of minor and major betrayals by a governmental socialism that long ago chose sides'.[1] In fact, when social democrats were in power, as in France from 2012 to 2017, they did not implement the solutions contained in their programmes and even adopted the insistent discourse of tax reductions. They made do with adjustments that did not reverse the pattern of inequalities. The presidential terms of the Democrat Obama proceeded from the same logic, and had a qualitatively similar outcome.

This pragmatism is all the more entrenched in that reinvigorating redistributive systems would require numerous technical obstacles to be surmounted. The retreat of the state as an economic actor locks it into a strategy resorting to tax incentives to try, in spite of everything, to construct an industrial policy; tax havens exist in all countries. Largely ineffective, these incentives open up the game of tax optimization that enables the most affluent and large numbers of big firms to determine the levels of tax they are prepared to pay.[2] The globalization of firms, fortunes and incomes, combined with tax competition between states, further enables the most powerful to choose the level of their tax burden.

In addition, the idea of a division of the population into 1 per cent versus 99 per cent is, in part, misleading. It corresponds to

---

1   Michel Pinçon and Monique Pinçon-Charlot, *La Violence des riches. Chronique d'une immense casse sociale* (Paris: La Découverte, 2013).

2   See Katia Weidenfeld, *À l'ombre des niches fiscales* (Paris: Economica, 2012).

a snapshot on a given date. During their life-cycle, a voter has a probability much higher than 1 per cent of one day figuring among the 1 per cent of highest incomes and fortunes. If she expects or hopes to enter this first centile in the future, she will be likely to support proposals for low taxation of the best-off.

At the other extreme of income distribution, support for social welfare and redistribution is far from automatic. The skill deployed by conservative forces to make the question of immigration the key political issue is not only electoral. As various works show,[1] the myth of the immigrant exploiting the welfare system[2] fuels hostility among 'popular strata' to instruments that largely benefit them. As for electorates whose majority comprises small property owners, they are worried by taxes on estates. I shall return to this.

Furthermore, the fear of being stigmatized as living on benefits is so marked that the take-up of various social benefits is sometimes low, as in France with the *Revenu de solidarité active* or in Germany with the *Sozialhilfe*. Poverty porn in advanced societies orchestrates this stigmatization, often inadvertently but sometimes deliberately; the British TV series *Benefits Street* was an example of this. In documentary mode, it claimed to portray everyday life in areas where virtually the whole population lived on social minima. It earned Channel 4 record audiences, thanks no doubt to its voyeuristic character.[3]

In this regard, the electoral success of a Donald Trump, with his promise to combine a revival of working-class America with cuts in social programmes, seems almost inevitable.

---

1   See Woojin Lee, John E. Roemer and Karine Van der Straeten, *Racism, Xenophobia and Distribution: A Study of Multi-Issue Politics in Advanced Democracies* (Cambridge: Harvard University Press/Russell Sage Foundation Press, 2007).

2   Let us recall that most numerical studies in OECD countries conclude that immigrants make a net contribution to welfare systems.

3   We may note that the TV channel M6 did not enjoy similar success with the French offshoot of this programme, *La Rue des Allocs*. This suggests greater sensitivity to fraternity on the part of the French.

The Cynics of Inequality

A glance at the activity of the International Monetary Fund (IMF) has the effect of persuading us of the cynicism of neoliberalism's promoters. The new leitmotif is 'inclusive growth'. After the OECD, and long after the International Labour Organization (ILO), since the mid 2010s the IMF has taken up the issue of inequality. Its research service is now at the forefront on this theme. The IMF has 'discovered' what 'heterodox' economists have been saying for years: inequalities are vectors of macroeconomic instability and even lower growth; or again, de-unionization encourages a growth in inequality. In an initial note on the subject dating from June 2015[1] – using methods as weak as the one employed by the IMF to explain that austerity would restore prosperity in Greece – IMF economists argued that an additional share of income obtained by the higher quintile would hamper economic growth. The authors summarized things thus: 'When the rich get richer, benefits do not trickle down.' In an apparent Copernican revolution for an institution that had long been a pillar of the theory of trickle-down, the IMF could now claim to be concerned with inequality. A splendid mirage!

In the Greek crisis of 2015, the IMF pushed for a restructuring of the debt, which it knew to be completely unsustainable. However, like the ECB and the European Commission, it demanded that Greek 'reforms' essentially take the form not of tax increases on the best-off, but of deep cuts in public services and social security – particularly pensions. The IMF's stance was even clearer in the case of Portugal. It saluted privatizations and public–private partnership schemes bound to accentuate inequality, before the Portuguese ushered in a new socialist majority supported by the communists.

'Structural reforms' of the labour market remain its obsession, like Matteo Renzi's Job Act in Italy, one of the breeding-grounds of

---

1   Era Dabla-Norris, Kalpana Kochar, Nujin Suphaphiphat, Frantisek Ricka and Evridiki Tsounta, 'Causes and Consequences of Income Inequality: A Global Perspective', staff discussion note 15/13, available at imf.org.

the arrival in power of the Cinque Stelle–Liga coalition. A Job Act of this kind is precisely what the election of Emmanuel Macron has ensured in France. Implementation of virtual employment at will,[1] abolition of taxes on transferable wealth, cuts in the finances of local bodies or the abolition of civil service posts – these certainly warranted both the enthusiasm of the IMF in its first report of July 2017 on France and the 'immense hope' of the general secretary of the OECD in September 2017. These institutions had not anticipated that, scarcely a year later, the Yellow Vests would convey their utter despair at a man who had become the 'president of the rich'.

For Another Way

Supporters of greater redistribution now face an impasse. Another approach consists in re-examining the primary allocation of income. Is it so natural? We shall see in the following chapters that it is very largely a construct. It can therefore be undermined, even replaced, by a different allocation on new theoretical and social bases. Before conducting this exercise, it is useful to recall the dimensions of the primary distribution of income.

To redistribute is not to distribute. I have already mentioned it in connection with income from benefits, and will return to it when I discuss the relevance of a universal basic income. Primary income possesses a much greater dimension of individual and social esteem than secondary income. To have a primary income of €1,200 and pay €200 in tax is not the same as earning €600 plus €400 of social benefits. Recent work on satisfaction and well-being underlines this. For example, using the remarkable German socioeconomic panel (SOEP), econometric studies[2] have

---

1   The ceiling on industrial tribunal damages makes it possible at very low cost, particularly in the case of employees with less than a year's experience, to lay workers off without a genuine and serious reason – for example, by invoking a fictitious grave infraction – and without warning.

2   Sonja Kassenboehmer and John Haisken-DeNew, 'Social Jealousy and

shown that the extra income obtained through the benefits system improves satisfaction, but by 50 per cent less than if it were an increase in primary income. Likewise, using the same survey over more than twenty-five years, other work[1] observes that the fact of paying taxes partially compensates, at the level of indicators of well-being, for the loss of secondary income occasioned by the taxation. To pay one's taxes demonstrates one's usefulness to the collective and participation in the common good. In other words, redistribution doubtless reduces monetary inequalities, but it does not diminish the dissatisfaction bound up with primary income.

The recognition afforded by primary income emerges clearly from studies of work. Economists and sociologists have shown that employees compare their wages with those of their colleagues or other occupational categories. This comparison has a direct influence on their satisfaction in work.[2] It is striking that wage-earners throughout the OECD do not take up certain social benefits, but instead embark on industrial disputes to secure increases involving sums much lower than those benefits. In occupational psychology, the wage is one component of recognition at work: it is the monetary value of my work, what I am worth. And the lack of recognition is a proven psycho-social risk.[3] Combined with onerous job requirements, it has multiple harmful effects on mental and physical health.

The issues bound up with working conditions demonstrate that inequalities cannot be consigned to a strictly monetary approach.

Stigma: Negative Externalities of Social Assistance Payments in Germany', *Ruhr Economic Paper*, no. 117 (2009).

1   Alpaslan Akay, Olivier Bargain, Mathias Dolls, Dick Neumann, Andreas Peichl and Sebastian Siegloch, 'Happy Taxpayers? Income Taxation and Well-Being', *IZA Discussion Paper* no. 6999 (2012).

2   On France, for example, see Christian Baudelot, Damien Cartron, Jérôme Gautié, Olivier Godechot, Michel Gollac and Claudia Senik, *Bien ou mal payés? Les travailleurs du public and du privé jugent leurs salaires* (Paris: Les Éditions d'Ulm/Cepremap, 2014).

3   See the founding article by Johannes Siegrist, 'Adverse Health Effects of High-Effort/Low-Reward Conditions', *Journal of Occupational Health Psychology* 1: 1 (1996).

Returning to the primary level has the advantage of embracing monetary forms of inequality, along with inequalities in living and working conditions, in order to reveal their common springs. This requires us to unpack, step by step, the mechanisms at work in contemporary economies. The first step is to identify the source of rents. The second consists in understanding how, and by whom, they are appropriated, and who pays the price.

2

Capitalism Unbound

Returns on capital, generous remuneration of a minority, and inadequate pay for whole layers of the world of work are neither 'physical' constants of economics nor the reflection of some 'natural' order of the market economy. If inequalities have grown, the explanation is to be sought elsewhere than in a pseudo-natural primary distribution of income. In recent decades, the global economic cards have been radically reshuffled. Behind these very large changes lie concealed mechanisms that have led to a veritable emancipation of capital.

Three have proved especially powerful. At the end of the twentieth century, the collapse of the Soviet bloc liberated vast spaces for rents, while abolishing a fundamental threat to capitalists. At the same time, the decline of trade unions and the de-structuring of the wage-earning class liberated rents that labour had garnered over the course of a century. In addition, for nearly three decades, technological waves, as well as the spatial agglomeration of economic activities, have created major new sources of income, while squeezing those of actors in the old economy.

The Fall of the Berlin Wall: From the New Europe to the New China

The fall of the Berlin Wall in November 1989 was a geopolitical and economic earthquake. It reconfigured the global economy from East to West and North to South. The first to be affected by the shock were obviously the countries of the former Soviet bloc. The latter were broadly more egalitarian than those of the West and most non-communist developing countries – despite the existence of an oligarchy. Value creation and related profits were very real, but were controlled directly by the state or by state enterprises. To a very large extent, the state fixed the level of everyone's primary income in accordance with status (academic, worker, pensioner). Thus, the transition of these economies, and their integration into trade relations with the West, enabled the manifestation of latent rents and abolished the state distribution of wealth.

This dual transformation translated into an explosion in inequality. According to World Bank data, scarcely nine years after the fall of communism the Gini coefficient (which measures inequality in disposable income) had increased from 0.24 to 0.33 on average in the former countries of the Soviet bloc.[1] As in the West, the new market economies created a wide disparity in people's pay, social position and opportunities, which could be seized by a minority able to prosper in dislocated societies characterized by marked tolerance for inequalities. But if, at the outset, growing inequality was experienced as proof of new opportunities, such tolerance was progressively eroded with the stratification of society.[2]

The liberation, followed by the appropriation, of rents was especially pronounced in countries in transition that implemented

---

1   See Branko Milanovic, *Income, Inequality, and Poverty during the Transition from Planned to Market Economy* (Washington, DC: World Bank Group, 1998).

2   Irena Grosfeld and Claudia Senik, 'The Emerging Aversion to Inequality', *Economics of Transition* 18: 1 (2010).

vast privatization programmes.[1] The case of Russia, and to a lesser extent that of Ukraine, is emblematic, in a context of kleptocracy, of the emergence of a powerful oligarchy that owns the bulk of the country's productive and energy apparatus. Further to the west, the option was available of a big bang to transform socialist economies into market economies at a stroke. In 1990, Poland under the supervision of Leszek Balcerowicz and the Czechoslovakia of Václav Klaus initiated vast reform programmes very largely inspired by the policies imposed on Latin America at the time by the IMF. Governments even anticipated the requirements of the Washington-based institutions, prompted in this by a procession of Western economists who were supposed to teach market economics to the new rulers. The prospect of future entry into the European Union encouraged an opening up of the sale of the most profitable state enterprises to Western financial powers. The standard profile of the purchasers would be national entrepreneurs supported by foreign investors.

In the West, the integration of the former countries of the communist bloc exacerbated the erosion in the position of workers. Several factors were operative. The first was the relocation of activities to the east – all the more rapid given that those countries were steered to join an expanded European Union in the medium term.

---

1   See Nina Bandelj and Matthew C. Mahutga, 'How Socio-Economic Changes Shape Income Inequality in Central and Eastern Europe', *Social Forces* 88: 5 (2010); Gianluca Grimalda, David Barlow and Elena Meschi, 'Varieties of Capitalisms and Varieties of Performances: Accounting for Inequality in Post-Soviet Transition Economies', *International Review of Applied Economics* 24: 3 (2010). Privatization processes in Western Europe were also often marked by conflicts of interest. France was particularly affected. Many directors of privatized companies were merely civil servants installed by the state to organize these privatizations. During the first vast privatization wave in 1986–88, the Chirac government even reserved part of the capital for industrial and financial enterprises managed or owned by supporters of Chirac and his party, on the pretext of constructing stable cores of shareholders. Conflict of interests also occurred during the 2008–09 financial crisis, when those charged with the public rescue of certain banking establishments soon entered the top management of these state-aided companies.

In 2004, the EU grew at once from fifteen to twenty-five members, becoming twenty-eight in 2015. This phenomenon was more complex than it first appears. Much of the foreign investment in the new Europe did not derive from relocation, but represented a response to the needs of local development. However, particularly in manufacturing industry, there was indeed a reconfiguration of the production chain. Only a small proportion of a car assembled in Germany or France is German or French. In the case of Germany, which is particularly implicated on account of its geographical position, the segments with less value-added tend to be made in the east, whereas those with high value-added are still produced in the west.

The impact of this on job opportunities and wages in the west is ambiguous: some types of jobs are in decline while others, at first glance better paid, are expanding. For example, in the border regions between Bavaria and the Czech Republic, we do not observe any reduction in wages in the western part. If the workers of the west are not necessarily losers in this process of organizing production over the European continent, the rents generated in the east benefit the totality of firms operating or producing in those economies.

A second factor in the weakness of workers was mobility within the European Union, which increased competition between them.[1] Examples of wage optimization by enterprises include the massive employment of workers from the east in meat-processing in Germany, or the replacement of France by Poland as the principal flag of road freight transport in Europe. The most significant from a macroeconomic point of view is the phenomenon of posted workers,[2] who account for around 1 per cent of total employment in Germany and France.

---

1   In contrast to the reception of refugees: either their number is modest, as in the UK or France, or large, as in Germany. But, either way, their integration into the labour market will be very gradual in a favourable demographic context.

2   Posting was established by European directive 71 of 1996, incorporated into bodies of national legislation just before the entry into the EU of

Compounding the dynamic peculiar to the new Europe and the Community of Independent States (incorporating nine of the fifteen former Soviet republics) is the Chinese giant. Confronted with the USSR, it is highly unlikely that communist China would have orchestrated such a rapid and pronounced de-socialization of economic rents and concentration of capital, leading to the emergence of so many great fortunes. Let us recall that China's major economic turn dates from 1992. The new slogan promulgated by the Fourteenth Congress of the Communist Party was the creation of a 'socialist market economy' with 'Chinese characteristics'. The initial reforms were radical: privatization of housing and abolition of the *danwei* (work units) that guaranteed lifetime employment and broad social security. The reform programme and opening up would continue relentlessly, moderated in the last decade by the emergence of regulated labour contracts[1] and increases in minimum wages.

As in eastern Europe, this opening up supplied drivers of growth for large Western multinationals. But they were much more powerful in the latter case, and the opening applied to much larger markets – from China, via India or South Africa, to Brazil. China's adhesion to the WTO in November 2001 created gigantic sustainable sources of income. The process of (out)sourcing of economic activity prompted by this opening was likewise on a much grander scale than anything associated with eastern Europe. Recent studies of the case of the United States suggest that the impact of outsourcing on employment there was undetectable in

---

the first countries from the east. A worker is regarded as 'posted' if she works in a member-state of the European Union because her employer has sent her to work in that member-state temporarily. If a member-state provides for minimal conditions of employment – such as a minimum wage – then these must also apply to workers posted to this state. This does not prevent 'social dumping'. In the case of a minimum wage, for example, it will indeed be paid to the wage-earner; but the social contributions will be those of the worker's country of origin, and hence are often much lower.

1   See, for example, Xiaoying Li and Richard B. Freeman, 'How Does China's New Labour Contract Law Affect Floating Workers?', *British Journal of Industrial Relations* 53: 4 (2014), pp. 711–35.

Table 2.1 The Ten Countries with the Most Resident Billionaires in Dollars according to Hurun Global Rich List 2019

China	658	Switzerland	77
United States	584	Russia	59
Germany	117	Brazil	53
United Kingdom	109	Thailand	50
India	104	France	48

Source: Hurun Global Rich List, accessed 26 June 2019.

the closing decades of the twentieth century, and only became apparent with the bursting of China onto the scene in the 2000s.[1]

In parallel, the concentration of wealth in the hands of appropriators of rents was globalized. This is conveyed by the famous lists of the global rich, and of countries with the largest number of billionaire residents (Table 2.1). In early 2019, the Hurun Global Rich List and Forbes put the boss of Amazon, Jeff Bezos (prior to his divorce), in first place, with his fortune of more than $100 billion – far ahead of the fourth-placed, and first non-American, the Frenchman Bernard Arnault, whose fortune amounted to 'only' $76 or $86 billion. In China, resident billionaires have proliferated. According to the 2019 Hurun list, 'Greater China' (China including Hong Kong and Taiwan) and India occupy first and fifth places among the global purveyors of billionaires. The sanctions against Russia in the wake of the Ukrainian crisis have reduced the number of resident Russian billionaires to 'only' fifty-nine, to which we must add the dozens of Russians installed abroad, particularly in the United Kingdom.

---

1   See, for example, Avraham Ebenstein, Ann Harrison and Margaret McMillan, 'Why Are American Workers Getting Poorer? China, Trade and Offshoring', in Lional Fontagné and Ann Harrison, eds, *The Factory-Free Economy: Outsourcing, Servitization, and the Future of Industry* (Oxford: Oxford University Press/CEPREMAP, 2017).

Capitalism Freed from the Mirror of Communism

If the set of purely economic mechanisms that followed the fall of the Berlin Wall is a major consideration, the key factor for the former Western bloc probably lies elsewhere. Basically, the collapse of European communism changed the political situation.

In the European countries that still had strong (albeit declining) communist parties, such as Italy and France, the 'red scare' definitively disappeared. The European Community had constructed new rights for workers, particularly in relation to working conditions (maximum length of the working day, and so on). The European Union that replaced it in 1992 was able to adapt itself to the all-consuming market. The veil that had been drawn to conceal the crude mechanics of capitalism lost its utility. It was no longer necessary for capitalists to make concessions to trade-union organizations. Even in countries vaunting anti-communism – foremost among them the United States – the claim that society is based on a large 'middle class' was no longer required to project an attractive image compared with the post-Stalin USSR (see Chapter 5).

In response to these arguments, it might be said that coincidences in dates do not amount to causes. While statistical science is largely irrelevant on this issue, political and historical analysis is illuminating.

One fact that speaks for itself is this: the blocking of the ILO supervisory process occurred a few years after the fall of communism. The ILO is, in fact, a concentration of industrial relations globally. In 2019, it had 183 member-states. Its structure is tripartite: the executive bodies comprise representatives of governments, employers and workers. Founded in 1919 under the auspices of the Versailles Treaty,[1] and now a branch of the United Nations, the ILO is over one hundred years old. Within

---

1   'Whereas the League of Nations has for its object the establishment of universal peace, and such a peace can be established only if it is based upon social justice'.

the International Labour Conference, also known as the international parliament of labour, each member-state is represented by a delegation composed of two government delegates, one 'employer' delegate, and a 'worker' delegate, each of whom has a vote. These delegates elect the representatives on the governing body by college, except for the principal global economies – the United States, China, Japan, Germany, the UK, France, Brazil, India, Italy and the Russian Federation – which have permanent members.

The ILO is known to the wider public for the definition of unemployment associated with the International Labour Office, the ILO's permanent secretariat. But, beyond statistical issues, the ILO's mission is to promote 'social justice and internationally recognized human and labour rights'.[1] It pursues 'its founding mission that labour peace is essential to prosperity' by promoting rights at work and reinforcing social dialogue to resolve problems relating to the world of labour.

The ILO supervises respect for these conventions by member states.[2] To guarantee neutrality, a panel of experts pronounces on the cases brought before it and on the interpretation of conventions. Next, a tripartite committee selects which expert observations should be retained. The selection has to win support within the colleges of each of the parties. During this stage, one of the three parties can therefore block the operation of the institution. This process involves all the countries that are signatories. The 'developed' countries are not immune from ILO observations.[3]

---

1   Presentation of ILO on the website of its journal *International Labour Review*, at onlinelibrary.wiley.com.

2   Francis Maupin, 'The ILO Regular Supervisory System: A Model in Crisis?', *International Organizations Law Review* 10 (2013).

3   Thus, in 2007, following a referral by the French trade union Force Ouvrière, the ILO concluded that the creation by the Villepin government of 'the new hire contract' was contrary to its conventions (in particular no. 158), because it allowed for dismissal without giving the employee any reason. The report by the director general of the ILO, dated November 2007, is available at ilo.org. The contract was definitively abrogated by a law of June 2008.

Let us return to the Cold War. Employers and unions in the West formed a coalition.[1] For employers, it was a question of blocking the entry of representatives of state enterprises from the Soviet bloc. Above all, they regarded the development of workers' rights – particularly free trade unions and the right to strike – as a tool for destabilizing the Soviet states and a means of projecting the image of a progressive capitalism confronting a conservative communism.

The instrumentalization of the ILO against communism became flagrant in 1980. In August, workers at the Polish naval shipyards of Gdansk went on strike. Their main demand was for free trade unions. They based their claim on convention no. 87 of the ILO on trade-union freedom, ratified by Poland in 1957. An extensive interpretation of trade-union freedom was then supported by a broad coalition: the college of Western employers, many employee representatives, and the totality of Western countries. Thus, the ILO immediately recognized the legitimacy of Solidarność (Solidarity), the first independent trade union in the Soviet bloc. This historical act contributed to the collapse of communism.

The British position at the time was a complete travesty. Even as Margaret Thatcher, who had just arrived in power, was preparing a legislative and repressive programme to drastically reduce union representation and the right to strike in the UK, she supported Solidarność. With the fall of the Berlin Wall in November 1989, Thatcher wanted to have done with the ILO, which compelled her to limit her policy of curbing the right to strike and other anti-trade-union policies. She wanted to denounce the ILO conventions formally. Anxious about the disastrous impact of this decision on Britain's image, employers in the Confederation of British Industry engaged in strenuous lobbying of the Conservatives to avert an unduly hasty exit from the ILO. Thatcher's forced departure in November 1990 ultimately buried this plan.

---

1   Jean-Maurice Verdier, 'Débat sur le droit de grève à la Conférence international du travail', *Droit social* 12 (1994).

Within the ILO, following decades of collaboration with trade unions in the West, the employer party very gradually altered its position after the fall of the Berlin Wall.[1] In 2012, it triggered an institutional crisis by blocking the supervisory process. The objective of the 'capitalist international' was to see to it that the interpretation of ILO conventions abandoned any recognition of the right to strike the world over, because it was particularly detrimental to multinationals. It now rejects the legitimacy of the committee of experts it firmly supported in the past against the communist bloc.

In some countries, employers no longer conceal their hostility to the conventions signed prior to the Soviet collapse. Thus, in France, Pierre Gattaz, president of Medef (the main employers' organization) demanded denunciation of convention no. 158 on the termination of employment in late 2015.[2] Mitterrand's France had ratified it in March 1989, a few months before the fall of the Berlin Wall; it has not been ratified since by any of the world's ten principal economies.

The fall of European communism and the transformation of China have therefore accentuated the dynamic of inequality and the domination of capital. But there is no point succumbing to nostalgia for a vanished bipolar world. On the contrary, these changes oblige us to construct new defences to protect the 'labouring masses' within a democratic framework.

The Weakening of the Trade-Union Movement and a De-Structured Wage-Earning Class

This task is all the more necessary because, at the same time, one of the historical defences against capitalist offensives – trade

---

1   Maupin, 'ILO Regular Supervisory System', describes the evolution of its discourse and actions.

2   A Member which has ratified this Convention may denounce it every ten years. The last window was from November 2015 to November 2016; the next will only open in November 2025.

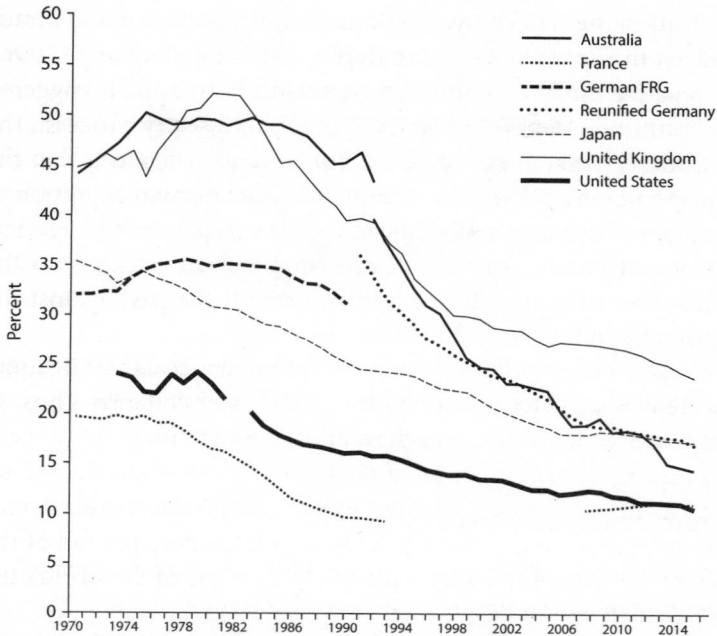

Figure 2.1 Rate of Unionization in Selected OECD Countries (1970–2016) as a Percentage

Source: OECD statistics for Australia, Germany and Japan; BLS (current population survey) for the United States on 7 January 2019. DARES estimates based on the number of trade-union dues 1970–93 and author's calculations from ERCV-SILC 2008–16 for France.

unionism – has become ever weaker in the wealthiest countries. This erosion commenced in the 1980s, and has extended to most of the major Western countries. It is expressed in a fall in rates of unionization and of collective agreements – that is, the percentage of wage-earners covered by a collective agreement negotiated between employers and employees' representatives.

The erosion of unionization rates – the percentage of employees belonging to a trade union – is quasi-general (Figure 2.1). It is pronounced in Anglophone countries where unions formerly enjoyed a large membership, like Australia, Britain, New Zealand and Ireland. It is also found in continental Europe, even in the lands of ordoliberalism such as Germany or Austria.[1] Asia – Japan and South Korea alike – is no exception. It is also the case in countries where the level of union membership was initially low, such as France and the United States. The Hispanic world, from Spain to Chile, exhibits some resistance, but remains well beneath 20 per cent membership. Even the Poland of Solidarność has experienced a collapse in the unionization rate, from 36 per cent in 1990 to 12 per cent in the 2010s. The regression is even starker in other countries of the new Europe: from more than half to less than 11 per cent in the Czech Republic and Hungary. Only a handful of 'small' countries,[2] where unions institutionally guarantee stronger social protection to their members (such as supplementary unemployment benefit), retain high rates of unionization.

Loss of identity and flexibility

Several complementary factors have been adduced to explain this phenomenon. The first is historical. The trade unions built since the late nineteenth century on a working-class, masculine identity are said to have proved incapable of adapting to the accelerated tertiarization of the economy, the feminization of the world of work, and the rise of management and professional occupations. But this argument is weak, because for the most part unions have proved adept at changing their spots, or new trade-union organizations have emerged. In Germany, the services union Ver.di (Vereinte Dienstleistungsgewerkschaft), created in 2001, has as many members as IG Metall, created after the Second World War. In France, the managerial union – Confédération générale des

---

1   Ordoliberalism is a liberal doctrine born in Germany in the 1930s that inspired the post-war German model. The state has an ordering role, guaranteeing a normative framework that ensures free, undistorted competition. Its fiscal policy must be balanced. Monetary policy specifies an independent central bank, and wages are fixed through joint negotiations between employers and trade unions.

2   These countries – Scandinavia (Norway, Finland, Denmark, Sweden), Iceland and Belgium – are smaller, combined, than the French economy.

cadres – is one of the five large confederations, and the others have management sections.

The labour economist Richard Freeman also maintains that new struggles over climate change, biodiversity or, more generally, anti-globalization, have eaten into mobilization on behalf of labour and contributed to the erosion of trade unionism.[1] However, most environmentalist movements regard less intensive work and less inequality as factors mitigating exploitation of the planet, and advocate a convergence of struggles. But it is true that such convergence remains largely potential, perhaps because it aspires to be non-ideological, as can be seen in the beginnings of the youth movement to defend the climate.

In addition, technological and organizational changes have created new obstacles to trade-union organizations. The imposed flexibility of working hours, the reduction in work breaks, the organization of work in short-term project teams – these result in the abolition of the casual periods when workers were able to meet at work and organize a collective. Technology is sometimes mobilized to eliminate social bonds even if the employer's initial goal is not necessarily to destroy bargaining power. Thus, to improve the cross-checking of employees, or to suppress the risks of chat, managerial software arranges a random attribution of hours and jobs on the checkouts in large food retailers.[2] The development of multi-tasking and job rotation finally blurs the construction of a common identity, which is useful for socializing shared problems and mounting collective struggles.

The splitting of the wage-earning class

To internal flexibility may be added an external flexibility – subcontracting in the workplace, with an increase in fixed-term

---

1   See, for example, his intervention, 'Les marches du travail européen et américain dans la crise', *Document de travail de la Dares* 189 (2015).

2   Philippe Askenazy, Jean-Baptiste Berry and Sophie Prunier-Poulmaire, 'Working Hard in Large Food Retailers', in Ève Caroli and Jérôme Gautié, *Low-Wage Work in France* (New York: Russell Sage Foundation, 2008), Chapter 6.

contracts and temping – that splits the wage-earning class even further. The large enterprise has not disappeared; but who is the struggle against when, in the same workshop or building site, wage-earners are dealing with multiple employers? The latter know perfectly well how to exploit this. The example of French nuclear power stations is striking: while the trade unions in the historical operators are still powerful, the bulk of the exposure to nuclides, particularly during site maintenance, is delegated to a multitude of subcontractors.[1] Similarly, site closures are a veritable anti-union weapon in the hands of employers, who can create competition between production or service sites, or prioritize closure of the most heavily unionized units.[2]

If technological as well as market factors have contributed to the decline of unions, public policy has accelerated it.[3] The general trend of privatization in western Europe facilitated a weakening of the bastions of trade unionism. Thatcherite policy was a success. Even more than the fall of trade unionism, it brought about a collapse in the numbers of those covered by collective agreements: from 70 per cent on Thatcher's arrival in power, it had fallen to 50 per cent by her departure, and to 30 per cent during the 2010s. This collapse allowed capital to recover the wage premium secured for workers by unionized structures.[4] Through a proliferation of

---

1   For the genesis of this human resources strategy in France, see Annie Thébaud-Mony, *L'Industrie du nucléaire. Sous-traitance et servitude*, INSERM collection, *Questions en santé publique* (2000).

2   Works by neoliberal economists confirm an increased risk of closure or job destruction in workplaces with trade unions. But they derive a different line of argument from this: these sites are sacrificed because they are less productive on account of the trade unions, or incapable of adapting on account of union intransigence. They conclude that trade unionism is harmful for wage-earners. See, for example, Francis Kramarz, 'Offshoring, Wages, and Employment: Evidence from Data Matching Imports, Firms, and Workers', in Fontagné and Harrison, *Factory-Free Economy*.

3   John Schmitt and Alexandra Mitukiewicz, 'Politics Matter: Changes in Unionisation Rates in Rich Countries, 1960–2010', *Industrial Relations Journal* 43 (2012).

4   Most studies show that the presence of unions is associated, all things being equal, with higher pay levels for employees. In parallel, studies of data on

derogation contracts, particularly in the part-time jobs mainly done by women, the Schröder government obtained the same result in Germany: collective agreement coverage, which stood at 90 per cent just after reunification, is now in the region of 60 per cent.

In some OECD countries, in the name of the fight against unemployment, the creation of individual enterprises has been made a priority. Millions of self-employed entrepreneurs find themselves dependent upon a purchaser in a relationship of de facto subordination. Other countries have allowed a hyper-precariat to flourish through a policy officially intended to facilitate recruitment. This is true of zero-hours contracts in Britain.[1] In France,[2] extreme simplification and digitalization of the administrative process now make it possible to hire workers in a few minutes; in some sectors, legal decisions recognize short contracts as the customary contract in place of permanent contracts. This has led to the signing of millions of contracts for less than a week. Every year in hospitality and catering, four times more contracts are signed than there are jobs! Moreover, although they are always legally protected by collective agreements, the employees concerned are in practice excluded from numerous provisions that are provided to workers after a minimum tenure within the company.

Thus, the fragmentation of the world of work into different 'statuses' – casual, contingent, self-employed, core worker, and so

---

profits suggest they are eroded, especially when the firm has a market position allowing it to extract significant margins from its customers. For a summary of work and debates on the issue, see Alex Bryson, 'Union Wage Effects', *IZA World of Labour* 35 (2014).

1   This is a contract without any guarantee of a minimum number of hours; workers are paid only for hours worked. According to the Labour Force Survey, the number of zero-hours workers is below 1 million. However, this figure massively underestimates the phenomenon. Using the business survey, the Office for National Statistics estimated that, as of November 2017, employers had issued 1.8 million 'non-guaranteed hours contracts'.

2   See Philippe Askenazy and Christine Erhel, 'Exploring the French Productivity Puzzle', in Askenazy, Lutz Bellmann, Alex Bryson and Eva Moreno Galbis, eds, *Productivity Puzzles across Europe* (Oxford: Oxford University Press/CEPREMAP, 2016).

on – has hitherto essentially been the result of public policy and the human resources strategies of businesses. This requires us to rethink the construction of the balance of power between subordinate workers and firms, which I will return to below.

The neutral employer of insider/outsider analyses

The fragmentation of the world of work should have been construed as a strategic act on the part of capital and neoliberal consultants, but has not been. In fact, attention has been diverted by the success of the so-called insider/outsider analyses, or the dualization of the labour market, initially developed by Swedish economist Assar Lindbeck and American economist Dennis Snower. What does it consist in? Part of the wage-earning class is said to be made up of insiders, who seek to protect their pay and jobs; trade unions are their mouthpieces. They prevent wages from reflecting individual skill levels, to adopt the terminology of the OECD, the IMF or the European Commission – an allegedly necessary condition for outsiders, casual workers and the unemployed, being able to access employment.

This view of the world of work has enjoyed considerable influence. It has prompted thousands of scholarly articles, particularly in economics and political science. It has inspired the political programmes both of conservative parties, for whom it justifies dismantling 'vested interests' – reducing the sphere of intervention by the state and its protected agents; and of social-democratic parties and trade unions, who make those excluded from the labour market their priority. Basically, the insiders/outsiders approach sets down a fable: unemployment and the precariat are the result of a conflict not between capital and labour, but between workers: between egotistical insiders and the outsiders who are their victims. Employers are merely neutral economic agents. Naturally, they seek to maximize their profits, but optimally they would like to employ as many people as possible. They simply want inequalities to reflect everyone's *natural* productivity. Unemployment would then be at its *natural* level.

In fact, the dominant microeconomic theories of the labour market over the last thirty years are based on this pseudo-neutrality. In the efficiency wage model, the enterprise is obliged to pay wages above 'competitive equilibrium'. It must do so to motivate employees – who by nature are *shirkers* – because it cannot fully control them. Worse, it must pay a wage premium that is all the larger because the wage-earner has an outside option (a safety net) in the event of the loss of significant work: unemployment or minimum welfare benefits. These 'extra costs' of labour ultimately create unemployment. In the matching theory, the enterprise dare not hire: it fears the costs of layoffs imposed by rigidities in labour law, or is frightened by legal uncertainty exacerbated by bureaucratic trade unions or nit-picking judges.

As for the powerful bosses' organizations and other lobbies present throughout the OECD and beyond,[1] their activities are simply ignored by the totality of mainstream analyses in the academic world and international institutions – or they are reduced to the status of neutral representatives of neutral employers. At the end of all theoretical equations and econometric estimates, we find no trace of the employer: all that remain are parameters defined by the worker's behaviour and by regulation. Consequently, these are recognized as the sole ills of the market economy.

From the New Economy to the Knowledge Economy

While the enterprise or employer is a neutral agent, capitalism has its heroes: from Apple to Facebook, these are the entrepreneurs of the new economy. Successful and not-so-successful Hollywood films are devoted to them. These self-made (wo)men are not only 'proof' that capitalism is not based on inherited wealth, but also symbols of an economy that offers progress for everyone.

---

1   Cofindustria in Italy, Medef in France, the CBI in the UK, BDA in Germany, Chamber of Commerce in the United States, KFI in South Korea, Keidaren in Japan, CII in India, CNI in Brazil, CCPIT in China, Business Unity in South Africa, and so on.

Behind this idyllic picture, the new economy and in particular the knowledge economy represent the other great transformation of contemporary capitalism. Beyond their impact on collective labour, they are the agents of a crucial part of the economic growth of recent decades.

Major waves in information and communications technologies (ICT) have succeeded one another: computerization in the 1980s; the internet and the network economy in the 1990s; mobility in the 2000s; the constitution and exploitation via social media of large masses of data – big data – in the 2010s. Here, too, the fall of the Berlin Wall served as a catalyst by accelerating the transfer of military technologies to civil applications, and by redeploying to them researchers and their associated resources. ICT has spread into numerous private and public economic activities, and is making rapid advances in performance for a stable or falling price.

ICT has become a key knowledge tool in all fields of knowledge and innovation. It helps to drive the dual trend of rising levels of employee qualification and progress in knowledge creation. The evolution of R&D expenditure is spectacular in most developed countries, with the notable exceptions of the UK and France. Initiated in the mid 1990s, this process has continued in the 2000s and now extends to the emerging countries (Figure 2.2). South Korea, with giants like Samsung and more than 10 per cent of the state budget devoted to research since 2008, has supplanted France. In the space of a few years, China has hoisted itself up to second place in the world, inexorably approaching the US giant.

In addition to enabling strictly technological innovation, ICT improves the performance of many activities, and is part of a mutation in work and occupations.[1] From the 1980s onwards, finance was the first industry to enter fully into the digital age, with the help of public investment and regulatory changes.[2] Machines

---

1   Philippe Askenazy, *Les Désordres du travail. Enquête sur le nouveau productivisme* (Paris: Éditions du Seuil, 2004).

2   Philippe Askenazy, *Blind Decades: Employment and Growth in France* (Berkeley, CA/London: University of California Press, 2015).

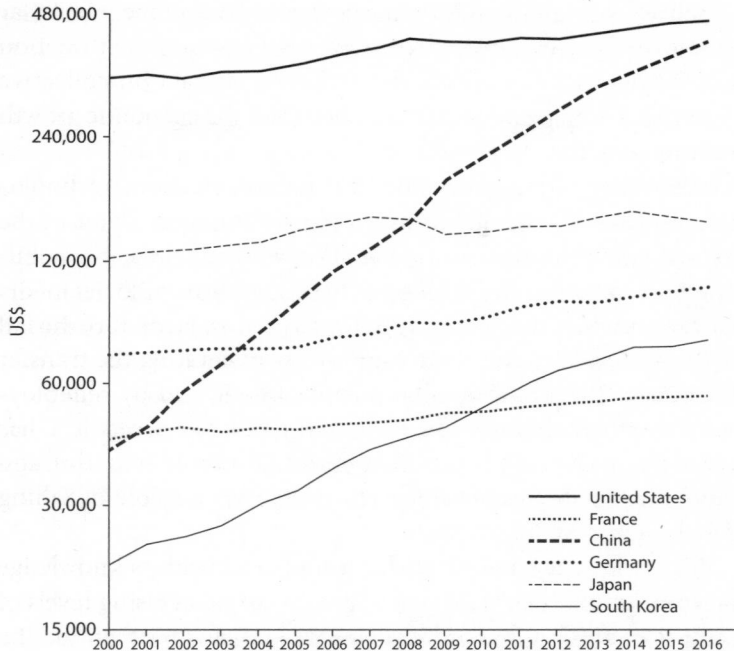

Figure 2.2 R&D Expenditure in the Six Largest Scientific Countries 2000–2016 (in 2010 constant dollars purchasing-power parity)

Source: OECD, main indicators for science and technology, on 8 January 2019.

Key: The six countries are those whose absolute R&D expenditure was highest in 2016. Logarithmic scale in base 2.

became able to perform a multiplicity of routine tasks in industry and the service sector. The apparent growth in labour productivity, particularly from the mid 1990s to the mid 2000s, was born out of the rise of forms of so-called high-performance work organization. From job rotation via just-in-time to total-quality management, such practices contribute to the intensification of work. The principle is to utilize the worker just as much in the cognitive sphere as the physical. Thus, blue-collar workers find new tasks being foisted upon them, such as customer management and quality control. The productive rents generated by the new economy are therefore not uniquely rooted in digitalization; they are also, or even especially, extracted from the bodies of workers (see Chapter 5).

Information technology also leads to an extension of the boundary of the enterprise. It facilitates the coordination of a multiplicity of suppliers and the globalization of trade. The extreme case is the industrial enterprise without a factory, in what is called the factory-free economy. On the one hand, the enterprise concentrates on innovation, marketing and commercialization while delegating production; on the other, the good produced is associated with a multitude of services invoiced to consumers. The world number one in capitalization – Apple – is paradigmatic of this schema. Even in the 'old' car-manufacturing sector, the major car makers have essentially become assemblers. They lower the prices of vehicles to realize margins on their offer of finance and maintenance.[1]

This is how a country without high-technology and active research sectors can enjoy an increase in growth through the use of ICT. The phenomenon is global, involving both developed and emerging countries, as well as underdeveloped ones. Its scale varies, however, with distance to the technological frontier.[2] Estimates for the OECD countries suggest that investment in ICT by enterprises and public agencies directly created around 0.5 per cent of annual economic growth in the first decade of this century (a slight drop compared with the 1990s), which represents a quarter of total economic growth over the period.

In addition to its impact on the productive sphere, the new economy has dramatically altered final consumption, destroying rents while creating new opportunities. The term 'disruption' captures these rapid swings. For many products, notably cultural ones, e-commerce has become normal. It dominates what

---

1   See p. 126.
2   See Maryam Farhadi, Rahmah Ismail and Masood Fooladi, 'Information and Communication Technology Use and Economic Growth', *PLoS One* 7: 11 (2012).

are called two-sided, intermediary markets that bring producers and consumers into contact. This is true of tourist activities,
particularly hospitality (Booking.com, Airbnb). Technological
goods themselves account for between 2 and 3 per cent of the
consumer basket, without counting all those integrated into other
goods (such as automobiles). In total, the sectors directly producing ICT goods and services for enterprises and consumers
account for between 5 per cent of GDP (in Spain) and 8 per cent
(in the United States), which nevertheless remains less than the
financial sector.

The nature of capital is also diversified in the new economy:
alongside machines and real estate (whether built or not), intangible or immaterial capital has become an essential factor of
production. It covers the information and knowledge held by an
organization. Three subcategories are generally distinguished:
digitalized information (software and databases, including big
data); proprietary innovations (designs, patents, financial services, rights in cultural goods, and even mineral exploitation
rights); and economic skills (market studies, advertisements,
organizational capital – for example, knowledge of efficient work
practices). According to the Intan Invest database,[1] investment in
intangibles by enterprises in the commercial sector has overtaken
their physical investment in many countries, including the two
principal European economies. In the case of the United States,
the phenomenon dates back to 1998; in 2017, its rate of intangible
investment stood at 15.2 per cent, as opposed to barely 10.6 per
cent for tangible investment.

---

1   See C. Corrado, J. Haskel, C. Jona-Lasinio and M. Iommi, 'Intangi-
ble Investment in the EU and US before and since the Great Recession and
Its Contribution to Productivity Growth', *Journal of Infrastructure, Policy and
Development* 2: 1 (2018).

The Agglomeration of Economic Activities

Along with the fall of communism and the industrial revolution around ICT, agglomeration is the third great force at work. The industrial transition of the emerging economies has automatically translated into a rapid advance in urbanization. The forces of agglomeration of economic activities reinforce this trend, driving a tendency towards spatial concentration. In the domain of innovation, agglomerations make it possible to group innovators, entrepreneurs, universities, and public research centres in the same location. Furthermore, enterprises sharing the same activity or complementary activities find suppliers whom they can share in one place, the latter benefiting from economies of scale. This might involve suppliers of goods or services – for example, air transport. The same applies to the labour force: enterprises unearth skills and workers find job opportunities in one and the same place. This translates into agglomeration gains – that is, enhanced performance by private and public employers. But the forces of agglomeration come up against congestion effects, which affect collective and individual urban transport in particular. Environmental constraints increase with atmospheric, water and sound pollution. Recent evidence also suggests that more densely populated cities have more-diffuse epidemics like influenza.[1] The case of Chinese megalopolises is an extreme example of the environmental harms that ultimately degrade the drawing power of towns and cities, from human health to productive efficiency.

In theory, the generalization of ICT would offer a response to this problem – for example, through remote working – and hence pave the way for de-concentration. In the most advanced countries, at any rate, globalization and the factory-free economy should also render agglomeration forces less significant. More generally, it is suggested that cities, particularly the most specialized, will experience a life-cycle of activities. The collapse of Detroit, the

---

1   For example, Benjamin Dalziel et al., 'Urbanization and Humidity Shape the Intensity of Influenza Epidemics in US Cities', *Science* 362 (2018).

historical heart of the US automobile industry, corresponds to this schema. Demographic ageing will add a supplementary centrifugal force, pensioners fleeing the metropolis and taking service jobs with them. 'Shrinking cities' should be nearly as common as growing cities in the OECD.[1] And yet, according to the latter's data, more than 85 per cent of metropolitan zones have seen their population density increase between 2000 and 2014. At the same time, academic works conclude that there are still significant agglomeration gains: when the job density of a zone doubles, productivity rises by between 2 and 10 per cent.[2]

The knowledge economy provides a first explanation for the agglomeration of activities and human beings. In fact, while the circulation of structured and planned formal information is liberated from distance, the informal information generated by physical proximity, even chance encounters, furnishes inputs that are sources of 'value creation' and innovation. In addition, the hyper-qualified and internationalized workforce of the knowledge economy is attracted by services – amenities – that are naturally found in greater number and variety in dense territories. This is true of cultural offerings (opera houses, theatres, museums), international schools for the children of workers, and airport hubs for leisure trips. Globalization, financialization, and use of ICT also encourage agglomeration: they oblige enterprises to resort to a multiplicity of services – marketing, finance, IT – supplied by concentrated, diversified poles.

The most pronounced example of this dynamic is represented by so-called 'global' cities – a notion popularized by American sociologist Saskia Sassen in 1991.[3] Since then, numerous classifications have appeared, with various logics. But all converge in

---

1   See Harry W. Richardson and Chang Woon Nam, eds, *Shrinking Cities: A Global Perspective* (London: Routledge, 2014).

2   Philippe Askenazy and Philippe Martin, 'Promouvoir l'égalité des chances à travers les territoires', *Note du Conseil d'analyse économique* 20 (2015).

3   See Saskia Sassen, *Global City* (Princeton: Princeton University Press, 1991).

broadly recognizing the same cities – more precisely, metropolitan areas – as compounding the advantages of the globalized economy.

We may begin with the most business-orientated classification – that of the GaWC (Globalization and World Cities Research Network), located at Britain's Loughborough University. It is based on data from surveys of the provision of services to enterprises (advice on strategy and organization, fiscal and legal consultancy, advertising, banking and finance). The bigger, more diversified and internationalized this supply, the higher the city's ranking. In 2010, the top two (in the Alpha++ category) were New York and London. In the category just below came Paris, Dubai and the Asian giants Tokyo, Hong Kong, Singapore and Shanghai. Most of the other classifications multiply the criteria to take account not only of purely commercial factors, but also academic and cultural provision, as well as political engagement. The 2018 ranking of global cities by A. T. Kearney thus places New York, London, Paris, Tokyo and Hong Kong in the top five – a hierarchy that has remained stable since 2012 (Table 2.2).

The phenomenon is not confined to the club of the wealthiest countries. Global cities flourish on all continents, from continental Asia – China in particular – to South America. They concentrate a globalized, mobile population, including a high proportion of immigrants and expatriates. In the same metropolis, pockets of extreme wealth may cohabit with a poor, ghettoized population. The latter supplies the armies of labourers required for the support roles – maintenance, commerce, transport, and so on – servicing enterprises, private individuals and local authorities.

The development of global cities can be described in further detail. The thirteen metropolitan areas of the OECD all experienced population increases between 2000 and 2014. Only Chicago and New York saw their density grow less rapidly than the federal average. Conversely, while the population in the rest of the country was in decline, Tokyo continued to expand. The population density of European capitals such as Brussels, Madrid, London and Amsterdam increased twice as fast as that of the rest

Table 2.2 'Global Cities' in the Second Half of the 2010s, Number of Billionaires in 2018, and Density and Weight for those in the OECD at the Start of the 2010s

	GaWC category 2016	Global Cities Index score 2018	Growth of population density from 2000 to 2014. In %	Percentage of EOCD GDP (2012)	Number of billionaires 2018
London	Alpha++	60.1	18	1,5	70
New York	Alpha++	62.0	4	2,8	92
Paris	Alpha+	53.2	10	1,7	36
Hong Kong	Alpha+	44.9			80
Tokyo	Alpha+	47.2	8	3,5	31
Singapore	Alpha+	37.8			31
Beijing	Alpha+	35.4			131
Shanghai	Alpha+	31.2			70
Dubai	Alpha+	(28)			18
Sydney	Alpha	32.5	19	0.5	18
Toronto	Alpha	31.7	30	0,6	14
Los Angeles	Alpha	38.3	13	2.1	24
Brussels	Alpha	34.3	15	0,3	0
Chicago	Alpha	36.3	6	1,3	14
Madrid	Alpha	33.2	30	0,7	14
Moscow	Alpha	32.7			62
Amsterdam	Alpha	29.3	14	0,3	4
São Paulo	Alpha	(31)			28
Mexico	Alpha	(38)	19		15
Milan	Alpha	(40)	8	0,5	14
Bombay	Alpha	(52)			55
Istanbul	Alpha	(26)			27
Jakarta	Alpha	(59)			16

Sources: GaWC (lboro.ac.uk/gawc, accessed 27 September 2018); A. T. Kearney 2018 Global Cities Report; author's calculations from the regional base of the OECD (9 October 2018); Hurun Global Rich list 2018. This table comprises the 'global cities' with a minimum of Alpha GaWC 2016 and among the twenty-five first GCIs or with at least ten billionaires in 2018.

of the countries concerned. Even if the data has some methodological limitations, it is clear that these same twelve metropoles
alone account for between 10 and 15 per cent of total OECD GDP.
If the dozen 'Alpha-cities' – Seoul, Vienna, Dublin, San Francisco,
Washington, and so on – are added, their combined share of GDP
approaches one-quarter. Paris, London, Brussels, Tokyo, Sydney,
Madrid and Mexico City each account for between one-fifth and
one-third of GDP in their respective countries; Seoul and the capitals of smaller countries, such as Dublin, account for nearly half.
However, part of this GDP does not correspond to the sphere of
the real economy. Financial activities, the headquarters of major
companies, and the wealthy all transfer into these world cities the
rents they extract from the national territory as a whole, and internationally. According to the Hurun ranking, New York has ninety
billionaires; London and Shanghai, seventy each; Bombay, fifty;
Paris, thirty – and so on.

States themselves fuel this accumulation. Brexit affords a good
example. European countries have fought one another to secure
the transfer of European agencies previously based in London to
their largest cities. Strategies are employed to attract the private
jobs, particularly in banking, that will have to migrate in order to
retain the European banking passport. One industrial priority of
Emmanuel Macron's France is to foster the role of Paris.[1] This takes
the form of pursuing a favourable environment for finance and
families from London: abolition of wealth tax, flat tax on financial income, reduction of taxes on financial activities, and so on,
as well as a doubling of the number of international state-funded
secondary schools in the Paris region (at a time when the number
of teachers in the country as a whole is set to fall).

Agglomeration thus creates wealth at the same time as it
leads inexorably to its spatial concentration. Primary distribution is thus mediated by geographical space, both within work
and between capital and labour. Finally, and crucially, it renders

---

1   See Philippe Askenazy, 'The Contradictions of Macronism', *Dissent*
(Winter 2018).

capitalism dependent on interactions between a large number of activities, and hence between occupations present in a few limited geographical zones.

In short, in a few decades market economies have experienced profound changes under the impact of geopolitical shocks, globalization, and mutations of a spatial, technological and organizational character. Fuelling one another, these have ended up creating or liberating significant rents. The deck of cards used in the economic game, broadly familiar over the century up to the 1970s, has been reshuffled or replaced. Beyond the new oligarchs, we now need to understand how certain economic agents, particularly in the historic countries of the OECD, have been able to pre-empt these rents by dominating the rules of the game. This domination is itself a catalyst of recent changes in market economies.

3

Propertarianism

The knowledge economy and the new economy should have led to a property and capital recession. Indeed, acceleration in the process of creative destruction depreciates whole swathes of capital. Increasingly, consumer durables wear out more quickly. Private individuals, as well as businesses and public bodies, now change their IT equipment with great frequency. Hardware increasingly represents a flow of expenditure, not an investment. It is rarer today for people to own an encyclopaedia, but they access a flow of information on the Internet. In this respect, Jeremy Rifkin was already evoking an 'economy of access' back in 2000.[1]

These new developments seem to condemn capital. However, its nominal growth and concentration have attained levels unequalled since the end of the Second World War. Whence this hiatus? Certainly, the lowering of taxes on the biggest incomes and fortunes has played its part. But it is only a consequence of a much more central factor: property and its appropriative capacity have been legitimated and extended. Even more so than capitalism, propertarianism in its two aspects – protection of property and desire for property – is predominant today.

1   Jeremy Rifkin, *The Age of Access: How the Shift from Ownership to Access Is Transforming Modern Life* (London: Penguin, 2000).

Two types of property are quite fundamental for the twenty-first-century economy: property in land and real estate, and property in knowledge. These are most apt to procure rents from agglomeration and the new knowledge economy. Public policy has largely supported their extension. As we shall see, propertarianism is not an isolated ideology: it forms part of a system with neoliberalism and cements the economic cohesion, hence domination, of conservative forces. Finally, propertarianism flags up new issues with the massive privatization of the information derived from digital networks.

The Return of Ground Rent

At the beginning of the nineteenth century, Ricardo advanced a theoretical framework for explaining the appropriation of rents by landowners through population growth. The latter implies an increase in agricultural output. On newly exploited land, however, returns are lower overall than those derived from land already in use, precisely because it is the most productive. At constant labour per acre of land (roughly 4,000 square metres), the cost of agricultural production increases. But, as the prices of agricultural products remain identical, the landowners with the highest returns collect a rent at the expense of consumers. Thus, when the population increases, it is the owners of the best land who benefit.

In urban economies, land is naturally a scarce resource, indispensable for both housing and economic activities. Its scarcity increases with growing population density – hence the rise in prices and transactions in the rental sector. The owners of the most agglomerated zones, or those that enjoy amenities often financed from the public purse, absorb the bulk of the extra remuneration associated with the presence and productivity increases of enterprises. Agglomeration rents are thus transformed into ground rents.

For a long time, this dynamic was counteracted. In many countries or cities, rents were controlled. This was true of France from

1914 until 1948, in particular to prevent the eviction of the wives of soldiers fighting for France, and then their widows, during the First World War. The development of transport made it possible, via urban sprawl, to mitigate land shortages.[1] We might add that the deindustrialization of the centres of large urban areas has freed up a vast amount of real estate, which can be reused to supply housing, shopping areas, museums, stadiums and offices. The archetype of this type of urban transformation is London's Docklands, which has become a financial centre now equipped with its incubators and accelerators for start-ups and the Tate Modern, converted from an old power station.

With rents that are no longer controlled, transport structures that have reached saturation point, and the industrial transition nearing its end, the curbs on ground rent have been lifted. To understand the mechanisms of urban ground rent, let us continue our investigations as economic tourists in our walk through London.

A spot of economic tourism

A distinctive system of real-estate ownership survives in Great Britain. In fact, two types of ownership exist for the same property: freehold or leasehold. The first involves ownership of the building and the land, possibly as a co-owner. In the second, a landlord is the owner of the ground and concedes the property for a very extended period – generally between 99 and 999 years – to a leaseholder. The leaseholder can resell this form of lease to someone else, who can sell it to another, and so on; she can also let the property. Several million British homes and enterprises are held by leaseholders. These 'sub-proprietors' pay a rent to the landlord. The level of this rent is fixed at the start of the concession, and is not indexed to price changes. Thus, with inflation, monthly instalments are very low in real terms for a lease that

---

1   Katharina Knoll, Moritz Schularick and Thomas Steger, 'No Price Like Home: Global House Prices, 1870–2012', *American Economic Review* 107: 2 (2017).

began, say, a century ago. On the other hand, leaseholders are obliged to pay maintenance costs on the property (the house or larger building) and its vicinity to landlords, who determine the annual sum. In a way, the leaseholder finds herself in the potential position of a co-owner whose co-ownership has been linked for centuries to the same property management company, which makes expenditure decisions on its own. Conflicts between leaseholders and their freeholder landlords are fairly frequent, and are arbitrated by English courts. However, a freeholder who is not unduly greedy receives a constant ground rent on his property without being disturbed by the risk of disputes.

In the absence of a revolution such as that of 1789 in France, entire districts of the city of London are still in the hands of aristocratic families. The most famous British estate, and one of the largest, is that of the Duke of Westminster, of the Grosvenor family. In 1677, Sir Thomas Grosvenor, a descendant of William the Conqueror, married Mary Davies and her hundreds of acres of land (fields situated a little to the west of the City). With the expansion of London, in the nineteenth century the Grosvenors established new districts that are today among the most prized in the world: Mayfair, Belgravia, Pimlico. The first two remain the property of the Grosvenors.

Let us continue our visit to the capital of the United Kingdom by plunging into the heart of the Marylebone district, between Hyde Park and Regent's Park. One hundred acres of this district, particularly Marylebone High Street, is the property of the estate owned by the Howard de Walden family. From the eighteenth century, it was built mainly on the basis of the plans of the architect John Prince. It aged badly: at the beginning of the 1990s, nearly one-third of retail spaces were vacant at a time when London was still booming. The estate decided on complete urban regeneration. It made buildings available to create schools and community activities, as well as a supermarket. These attracted well-connected families with high incomes, and a fashionable set of new shops. The area is now one of the most attractive in central London, with corresponding house prices. Thus, by improving the quality of the environment more than that of the properties themselves, the Howard de Walden Estate was able to reconstitute its ground rent. By attracting the best-off, these English families are able to divert a portion of the wealth created in London into ground rent.

If the case of London remains exceptional on account of its feudal legacy, the mechanisms at work are more general. The totality of global cities, taken together, offers an arresting illustration of stratospheric property prices. Alongside 'tax havens' like Monaco and Grand Cayman, these cities figure among those where real estate is the most expensive in the world (Figure 3.1). Bombay and Shanghai post real-estate prices (for a property in a prime location) above $10,000 per square metre, according to *Global Property Guide*. Since they do not own whole districts,

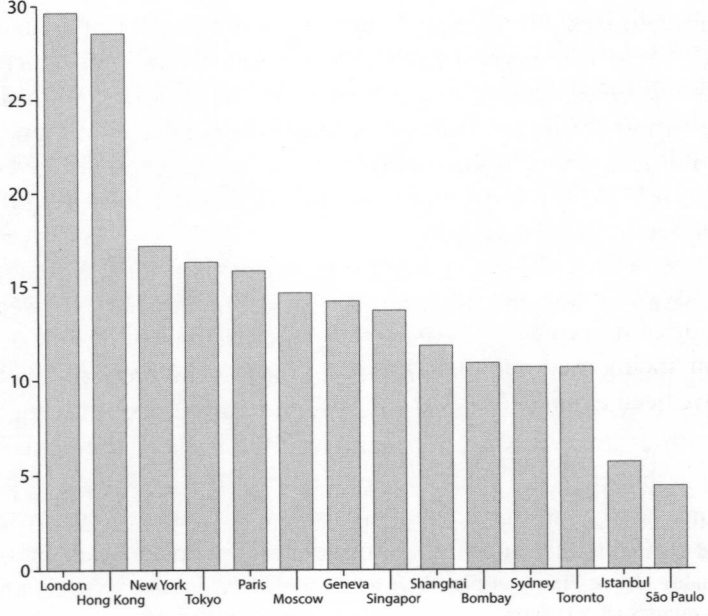

Figure 3.1 Price of Real Estate in Global Cities (price by square metre in thousands of dollars for 120 square metres, late 2017 or 2018)

Source: Global Property Guide. Most expensive cities (globalpropertyguide.com/most-expensive-cities, accessed 8 January 2019).

voters – owners as well as tenants – empower municipal majorities that plan urban regeneration and an improvement in amenities, further enhancing the attractiveness of these cities.

While the size of current rents can be measured, statistical demonstration of an increase in ground rent (housing or commercial real estate) over the long term nevertheless remains very difficult, even uncertain.

Has ground rent increased?

An initial argument often advanced is that, in many OECD countries, the price of residential property has experienced spectacular rises in the last fifty years – with rare exceptions such as Germany, which is characterized by demographic decline.[1] The property-price approach, although prioritized by many authors, is especially fragile. Data for the nineteenth century and the first half of the twentieth is fragmentary, often confined within the boundaries of the capital at the time. In addition, until recently, these indicators did not take account of improvement in the quality of properties.[2] If prices rise because properties have improved in quality (addition of a bathroom, a lift, and so on), this cannot be regarded as a sign of an increased ground rent. Thus, in France the widespread restoration of old properties, particularly in the city centres of Paris, Lyon and Lille in the 1980s and '90s, contributed to price movement in this period.[3] It is only more recently that convincing methodologies for assessing developments in quality have been employed.[4]

---

1   Ibid.

2   Work on the United States and UK suggests a very marked overestimate of the increase in property prices. See, for example, Patrick H. Hendershott and Thomas H. Thibodeau, 'The Relationship between Median and Constant Quality House Prices: Implications for Setting FHA Loan Limits', *Real Estate Economics* 18: 3 (1990).

3   For example, the transformation of maids' rooms into flats with all the mod cons.

4   Thus, in France, which is a leader in this field, INSEE data have only graded the quality of properties with a robust methodology since the late

A different approach consists in looking at the share of housing expenditure in household budgets. In sixty years this share has increased considerably in many countries, and more moderately in the United States. On average, it stands at more than 20 per cent in the OECD. Rents, implicit rents and interest on loans account for most of this. The sum of rents alone in national income is said to have quintupled between 1950 and 2010.[1] But, here too, numerous methodological problems arise in any effort to interpret this phenomenon before the 1980s. For example, during the first industrial revolutions, many employers provided accommodation at low rents – such as cottages for miners. These did not reflect a smaller rental income for the proprietor, but a mode of indirect remuneration. On the contrary, even, they marked the ascendancy of capital by immobilizing the labour force and rendering it dependent. This continued until the 1970s. In France, the case of Clermont-Ferrand's experience with Michelin is emblematic. The town's growth until 1975 mainly derived from the development of tyre factories and Michelin housing estates for its workers and their families. For these estates it had optimized, Michelin had demanded that 'the rooms ... be sufficiently large but not excessively so; tiring housework must be avoided'.[2]

In trying to assess movements in rents, it is therefore preferable to confine ourselves to a recent period. From the turning-point of the 1980s, rental indices take at least some account of the effect of quality. In addition, they make it possible to distinguish between certain geographical areas, particularly in the case of France and the United States. Comparison by area makes it possible to bring

1990s. For a presentation of the new methodologies, see Alain David, François Dubujet, Christian Gouriéroux and Anne Laferrère, 'Les indices de prix des logements anciens', *Insee Méthodes* 98 (September 2002) and 128 (July 2014).

1   Thomas Piketty, *Capital in the Twenty-First Century*, trans. Arthur Goldhammer (Cambridge, MA: Harvard University Press, 2014).

2   Extract from the *Cahier des charges du programme de construction des cités* entrusted to Pierre Boulanger after 1918. Quoted in Christian Lamy and Jean-Pierre Fornaro, *Michelin-ville: le logement ouvrier de l'entreprise Michelin 1911–1987* (Saint-Just-prés-Brioude: Editions Créer, 1990).

out more clearly the appropriation by real estate of a percentage of the rents created by agglomeration mechanisms. Thus, in France a marked real-terms rise in rents can be seen in conurbations of more than 20,000 inhabitants since 1978. In the period 2000–12, for which the data are presumably more reliable, rents rose particularly in the Parisian agglomeration twice as quickly (in constant euros) as in small and medium-sized conurbations (less than 20,000 inhabitants and 20,000–100,000 inhabitants – see Table 3.1).

Table 3.1 Rise in the INSEE Rental Index in Real Terms by Tranche of Urban Unit, 1978–2012 (as a percentage)

Less than 20,000 inhabitants	From 20,000 to 100,000	From 100,000 to 2 million	Paris agglomeration	All urban
12	27	28	28	25

Source: Jacques Friggit, *Loyers et revenus depuis les années 1970*, Mimeo of the CGEDD, from INSEE data, with 2000 as base.

Data for the United States likewise suggest divergences according to size of the zone considered. Since 1988, rents have risen much more rapidly in large conurbations (more than 1.5 million inhabitants). These averages conceal great spatial diversity. Thus, in Silicon Valley rents have soared, whereas they have fallen in the old heart of the US automobile industry of the Detroit region (Table 3.2). The overall rise in rents nevertheless remains more moderate than in France (less than 9 per cent in real terms over the same 1978–2012 period).

Table 3.2 Rent Increases in Real Terms for a Main Residence in the United States (as a percentage), Early 1988–Late 2018

Mean Urban	Less than 50,000 inhabitants*	More than 1.5 million	Detroit-Warren-Dearborn	San Francisco, Oakland, San Jose
+19	+6	+26	−3	+50

Source: Author's calculations from Bureau of Labor Statistics data (consulted 17 January 2019).

Note: Rent indices are deflated by the Consumer Price Index for All Urban Consumers.

Housing is only one area where ground rent is relevant. All productive activities are equally affected by a possible appropriation of their profits by the owners of real estate and buildings. Unfortunately, the methodological difficulties involved in calculating market prices – of capital as well as rents – are even greater when it comes to residential housing. Measurement of the quality of properties is very tricky. Worse, a significant percentage of rental flows occur via real-estate companies. Various mass retail giants, such as Walmart and Carrefour, have sold their properties to their own real-estate companies, which have become the owners of buildings they then let out to the group's retail chain at levels that are not necessarily economically meaningful. As a result, the data on property return from private companies like Investment Property Databank are too noisy to follow the evolution of business rents.

Only recently have major statistical institutions attempted to produce series on business rents: 2006 for Canada, 2009 for the United States, 2010 for France. They all exhibit a divergence between the rents of tertiary assets (offices, shops, hospitals) and the rents of industrial establishments, the former increasing while the latter have fallen. This 'scissors' effect is perfectly consistent with the rise of ground and building rents in zones where agglomeration mechanisms predominate.

All told, while it is difficult to assess the scale of the phenomenon, the (big) owners of land and buildings clearly seem to exploit the scarcity of their goods to procure a share of the rents created by agglomeration effects, at least on private individuals. Moreover, if the trend in the rent charged directly on buildings used by business is not currently quantifiable, the effect on employees of a rise in property prices is not neutral for those businesses. In fact, they must partially offset the cost of accommodation through wage increases.[1]

---

1   See Juan Carluccio, 'L'impact de l'évolution des prix immobiliers sur les coûts salariaux. Comparaison France-Allemagne', *Bulletin de la Banque de France* 196 (2014).

Propertarianism Reinforced

These increases ultimately fuel a cycle favourable to property owners, but also to the financial sphere. The latter is a double winner: on one hand, the large insurers have real-estate portfolios that increase in value, enabling them to consolidate their capital base; on the other hand, real-estate loans are all the more profitable because buying a home requires a significant, extended commitment. The opportunity to buy debt in the form of US subprime or Swedish interest-only mortgages further increases returns.[1]

Ground and property rent benefits not only from economic mechanisms, but also in many countries from tax regimes that encourage it. The latter reinforce a form of propertarianism – the desire to own one's home – that is thriving with the increase in life expectancy: enjoyment of ownership is lasting longer. This tendency represents a form of insurance for retirement, even dependency. An economic–fiscal–political circle is thus created, in which the base of real-estate ownership grows as citizens become the owners of their main residence.

Thatcherism sought to make citizens into shareholders who owned a little capital, bolstering the democratic legitimacy of capital for the benefit of the minority of capitalist citizens who were major shareholders. The apparent democratization of property and real-estate ownership derives from the same logic. It makes it possible to insulate property rights and an accommodating tax regime, including on inheritance, from political challenge. One of the major proposals of Britain's Conservatives during the 2015 election campaign was the possibility for tenants in the social-housing sector to acquire their residence with a 35 per cent reduction, in order to further cement propertarianism in the UK. This proposal played a part in David Cameron's success, especially among a section of the electorate that had not suffered any reduction in spending power during his premiership. As I indicated in

---

1   With an interest-only mortgage, the borrower only pays interest on the loan, reimbursing the capital sum borrowed on maturity.

Chapter 1, the proposals advanced to facilitate homeownership are scarcely a threat to the established order.

Since the middle of the twentieth century,[1] nearly two-thirds of North American householders have owned their homes. This proportion has remained relatively stable. By contrast, in Germany, France and the UK these proportions were still the reverse in the 1950s, with around two-thirds of occupants renting. With the exception of Germany, where the expansion of ownership of a main residence has been moderate, from the UK via the Netherlands to France there has been a clear convergence on the North American model; owner-occupiers now form the majority. The data of Eurostat's SILC survey enable us to draw up a picture for the European Union as a whole in 2017. All countries have a majority of homeowners, from 51 per cent in Germany to 96 per cent in Romania.[2] In France, nearly 64 per cent of householders are owners of their accommodation (a little less than 60 per cent according to INSEE's Estates survey). In eastern Europe, many householders remained owners of their accommodation at the moment of transition. The percentage of owners was below 65 per cent in 2017 in the former European Union of fifteen member-states, but over 80 per cent in the new member-states. The existence of high percentages of owner-occupiers – 77 per cent in Spain, for example – must, however, be qualified. These rates might also be indicative of a crisis in access to housing: the young cannot afford either to rent or to buy, and are compelled to remain at home with their parents. In fact, to a very considerable extent, the democratization of property ownership is a façade. Levels of ownership of a main residence, but also the characteristics of the

---

1   Greg Suttor, *Rental Paths from Postwar to Present: Canada Compared*, Cities Centre, University of Toronto, Research Paper no. 218 (2009). Covering a shorter period (from the start of the 1990s), but more countries, see Dan Andrews and Aida Caldera-Sánchez, *Drivers of Homeownership Rates in Selected OECD Countries*, OECD, Economic Department WP no. 849 (2011).

2   The proportion of owner-occupiers seems, however, to be slightly higher than that obtained in general by national studies. For example, 64 per cent for France as against 58 per cent in the INSEE study.

properties concerned (size, location, quality) and especially levels of ownership of several properties, are heavily dependent on levels of income and inherited wealth.[1]

All Is Property

While private ownership's ascendancy over real estate is visible to all, the knowledge economy might seem to escape it. The everyday use of the Internet is adduced as proof of this. With one click, the Internet makes it possible to access an infinity of content that is very often free for the surfer, even when it comes with advertising. Offered by giants like Google but also by start-ups, many apps are also available at no cost other than that charged by the service providers: Google maps, Doodle, Skype, Facebook, and so on. Better still, collaborative movements like Wikipedia offer content that is universal, multilingual and free (open source, open data). Beyond the Internet, they inspire a collaborative economy in numerous local activities facilitated by social media. From Gumtree in the UK to Bon Coin in France, a barter economy has been created between private individuals on the margins of the market economy. This new ecosystem has first benefited from the neutrality of the net – equal treatment of data flows on the Internet – which has become established in democratic countries at least, including the United States.

But property has not abdicated, as analyses carried out by specialists in the 'commons' reveal.[2] I am going to take up some of

---

1   If one takes the limit of 60 per cent of median income by unit of household consumption, SILC finds 43 per cent of owner-occupiers beneath this limit and 71 per cent above it in the Eurozone in 2017.

2   Regarded as forgotten or abandoned by liberal and Marxist authors alike, the analysis of common goods and the role of institutions was revived by the economic research inspired by Elinor Olstrom, *Governing the Commons: The Evolution of Institutions for Collective Action* (Cambridge: Cambridge University Press, 1990). Beyond economics, political scientists, philosophers and anti-globalization movements regard the commons as a theoretical basis for

their key elements without employing the theoretical concepts of this literature.

Let us return to the 1980s. The knowledge economy associated with the advance of intangible capital was set to become established. Already, ideas and knowledge – from cinematic films via patent licences to software programs – were seeing their share of world trade grow. Even in material goods, from medicines to branded footwear, value no longer derived decisively from raw materials.

At the same time, globalization was now underway. Protection of intellectual property was not guaranteed by multilateral accords. Under the impetus, in particular, of the United States, which already saw itself as the leader of the knowledge economy, negotiations began in 1986: the Uruguay Round. It would lead in 1994 to the creation of the World Trade Organization. The WTO Agreement on Trade-Related Aspects of Intellectual Property Rights (TRIPS) introduced detailed rules on intellectual property into the multilateral trading system for the first time. The agreement imposed convergence on these rights in the signatory countries, and their submission to common international rules. In particular, it fixed minimum levels of protection of intellectual property. The areas it covered were very diverse: authorial royalties, patents, designation of origin (champagne or tequila), brand names and trademarks, industrial designs – and even commercial secrets. For example, a sound recording is protected for fifty years. Only after twenty years does a patent expire, its object entering the public domain. Such protection extends even to the results of trials communicated to authorities with a view to approval of the marketing of pharmaceutical goods or crop-protection products. Not only can GMOs be patented; WTO agreements also stipulate that the signatories must provide for the protection of non-GMO plant varieties by patents – or by a *sui generis* system that makes use of plant variety protection certificates.

---

constructing an ideological alternative to neoliberalism or social liberalism, encompassing the totality of social and environmental issues.

The principle promulgated by the WTO is that states confer these rights on creators to incentivize them to generate ideas that ensure an 'increase in the economic and social welfare' of producers and users. But these property rights, particularly in patents, are restricted by the principle of competition. Thus, in certain circumstances, the agreement empowers governments to take measures to prevent anti-competitive practices as regards the granting of licences.

But economic theory, in common with empirical work, is unable to conclude that the globalization of intellectual property rights, even when restricted in this way, has in fact encouraged innovation, or ultimately growth. In fact, two mechanisms clash, making the WTO agreement deliberately one-sided. On one hand, rights effectively guarantee creators a remuneration that returns a profit on investment in new ideas. On the other, those same rights establish a privatization of knowledge, erecting monetary and technological obstacles to the creation of new knowledge. The holders of complementary patents can agree, sometimes after mutual threats of litigation, to bolster their own innovations – but only at the expense of new innovators. Such, for example, was the 'battle' between the two leading producers of smart phones: Apple in the United States and the South Korean Samsung. We shall return to this conflict.

Recent work suggests that the first mechanism dominated in the WTO's early years, but that the second caught up with it as the perimeter of knowledge was extended.[1] It was then affected by the stagnation in productivity that endured throughout the OECD for ten years. At all events, one thing is agreed: the protection of property rights in knowledge has clearly translated into an extension of the sphere of property.

To the extent that their ideas are capable of tapping global demand, property owners can draw sizeable rents from it. Even 'star' intellectuals profit from it. The author of the *Harry Potter*

---

1   For example, Ugo Pagano, 'The Crisis of Intellectual Monopoly Capitalism', *Cambridge Journal of Economics* 38: 6 (2014).

saga has become one of the wealthiest people in the United Kingdom, with a fortune estimated at nearly £500 million. A little more modestly, Choupette (born Guimauve du Blues Daphnée), couturier Karl Lagerfeld's Birman cat, whose Instagram account had 115,000 subscribers in late 2018, has racked up several million euros through lending out her image.[1]

But it is corporations and, behind the scenes, their public or family shareholders, who receive the bulk of these rents. The pharmaceutical domain is one of the best illustrations of this, inasmuch as it involves an essential dimension of human existence: health. At the beginning of August 2019, the four global giants – the Americans Johnson & Johnson (Imodium) and Pfizer[2] (Viagra), and the Swiss Novartis (Voltarene) and Roche (Lexomil) – each represented between 200 and 400 billion (in euros, dollars or Swiss francs) in terms of capitalization. For comparison, the Greek debt reached 'only' €320 billion during the crisis of 2015, and would have been readily sustainable had it been reduced by half.

The valuations of biotechnology firms are even more staggering. Less well known than their counterparts in IT, Gilead Sciences (virology) and Amgen (genetics) were valued in mid 2019 at between $80 billion and $120 billion on the Nasdaq – in the vicinity of the valuation of IBM. But these companies are very young. Amgen was created in 1980. Gilead, however, dates only from 1987. It was chaired by Donald Rumsfeld, prior to his becoming defense secretary under George W. Bush.

---

1   Even so, there were many fewer than the 5 million followers of her master prior to his death!

2   In November 2015, Pfizer announced the purchase of the Irish Allergan with an inversion: the new group would be based in Ireland, with its well-known tax sweeteners. In the end, the US Treasury under Obama, by imposing stricter rules on tax inversion, halted the process in April 2016: striking proof that the operation was motivated not by tax optimization rather than industrial strategy.

The Privatization of Information

The propertarianism I have described here is essentially a legacy of the last decades of the twentieth century. The new century has ushered in a supplementary form.

Let us return to the Nasdaq. Its highest capitalizations pertain to the ICT sphere. In early December 2018, the first- and third-placed – Microsoft and Apple – took full advantage of the intellectual property regime in all its dimensions (brands, logos, patents, software). Different, much younger actors became established in the space of a very few years: pure players whose activities and profits are almost exclusively generated on the Internet. We are talking about Amazon (created in 1994), Google (1998), Facebook (2004) and Netflix (2002), all of which have become global actors. The United States has no monopoly on the birth of giants: the Chinese Alibaba (created in 1999) and Tencent (1998), and, to a lesser extent, the Japanese Rakuten (1997), are just as powerful in Asia. At the start of January 2019, the Alphabet holding – Google – was, like Facebook, worth $700 billion, while Alibaba and Tencent stood at around $400 billion.

These actors surf on a 'new new' economy. They are joined in certain sectors (music platforms, videos) by older ICT firms, and even by traditional actors struggling to maintain their positions.[1] Their characteristics are as follows.[2] In the first instance, they are platforms that connect internet users with businesses; they are thus in economic terms, two-sided markets. Their value is all the greater when they have the opportunity to attract a very large number of surfers, and to offer them targeted advertisements. The supply of multiple free services has one aim only: attracting the maximum number of web users and extracting from them

---

1   One of the world leaders in hospitality, Accor, is thus trying to counter Booking.com and Airbnb by investing massively in its own platform.

2   The research report for France Stratégie by Maya Bacache et al., *Taxation and the Digital Economy: A Survey of Theoretical Models* (Paris: Paris School of Economics/Telecom Paris-Tech/Toulouse School of Economics, 2015), offers a comprehensive theoretical panorama for more specialist readers.

the maximum information about themselves in order to target these ads precisely. Classical network effects then do their job. Once a critical mass of surfers has passed through the platform, the latter can rapidly become a monopoly or part of an oligopoly. The power acquired makes possible investments that ensure the platform's technological supremacy. Thus, more than 90 per cent of search requests on the Internet in Europe go through Google. Google and Facebook's plans to guarantee Internet access on all continents through new infrastructure (stratospheric balloons and so on) do not correspond to some 'mission' of development aimed to reduce the digital divide, but to the extension of their network and their knowledge of human beings the world over.

Even from a purely neoliberal perspective, these actors are not unproblematic. The first problem relates, once again, to competition. Dismantling classic monopolies, which were often initially public, and frequently took the form of networks – such as telecoms, energy and rail transport – is easy. But when it comes to the giants of the net, the communication network – the worldwide web – is already open, and network effects are created by the subscription of actors to virtual platforms. The competition authorities – the European Commission in the case of Google – are therefore restricted to penalizing abuses: prioritization of its own products in search results, in the case of Google. The second problem is taxation. Multinationals know full well how, through transfer pricing, to decrease their profits in a particular country and increase them in others, where taxation is lower. In the case of platforms, the very notion of territory is quite simply voided.

These issues are obviously important, but the most fundamental one is the construction of privatized sources of knowledge involving virtually all dimensions of the individual – and this for the whole population: health, education, leisure, sexuality, jobseeking. Their nature and scale no longer have anything to do, for example, with a standard market survey, or even with a population census by a national statistical office. They also qualitatively and quantitatively go beyond the data collected on their customers by traditional businesses (for example, an insurer). Even if the tools of big data open up new prospects for the latter, they remain in the realm of optimization, and do not represent the accumulation of a new form of knowledge.

On the other hand, the databases of platforms, fed in real time, are the result of the depositing of information by millions of citizens or businesses – that is, a form of collaborative economy. Yet they are the exclusive property of the platforms.

To camouflage this exclusivity, while also rendering intellectuals and institutions dependent upon them, platforms skilfully construct collaborations. Google (Alphabet) has the most advanced version of this strategy. For example, it undertakes partnerships with libraries and archives for digitalizing collections now entering the public domain. Why does Google embark upon such private partnerships? Let us take one of the biggest digitalization agreements: the one concluded with the British Library for 250,000 works. Google is financing it all – but it demanded contractual confidentiality. The contract had to be disclosed when the Open Rights Group invoked English law on administrative transparency. One of the clauses imposed on the British Library was to reserve indexation of the full text exclusively to Google, utilizing technologies that blocked other research engines. In an apparent open-data initiative lay concealed both a surreptitious extension of Google's ownership of initially public materials and an assertion of its exclusivity.

Google's strategy of diffusing search statistics is equally remarkable. Research teams throughout the world, financed by funds both public and private (from outside Google), now use these data in numerous disciplines. In medicine, for example, by studying billions of searches by web users, one can draw up a panorama of medicinal interactions (number of times that drugs A and B feature in the same search) and side effects (backache for drug X, for example), and even discover new therapeutic applications. In economics, some researchers hope to construct more pertinent economic indicators; aided by French research groups, the OECD is constructing high-frequency indicators of well-being.[1] By involving researchers and decision-makers, Google is rendering itself increasingly indispensable. Moreover, it is thereby learning what might be done with its data when it ultimately amasses the relevant information. In fact, such research is conditioned by the quality, relevance and integrity of the information supplied by Google. These are all things that depend on Google's ownership algorithm and developments within it. This algorithm is the heart of Google's industrial secret – a secret that it guards jealously. In the end, Google alone can see the research through whenever, and with whomever, it likes.

Propertarianism, Neoliberalism and Authoritarianism

Following the historical thread, we find that conservative forces have played a crucial role in promoting the public policies that gave birth to propertarianism. At the same time, these conservative forces were in the service of neoliberalism. Seemingly distinct, the two ideologies are in fact economically complementary. Thus, as we saw in Chapter 2, two of the pillars of neoliberal policy – the privatization, or outsourcing and dismantling, of public services – automatically enable financialization and an extension of the domain of private property.

Neoliberalism and propertarianism increasingly pollute the non-market sector. The development of Public–Private Partnerships (PPP) amplifies this dynamic. A PPP consists in the mobilization by a public actor of private providers to finance and manage a facility delivering a public service: a hospital, a stadium, a prison, and so on. Invented in Britain in the early 1990s, this device has spread throughout the world, to the advanced and less advanced economies alike. The state and local authorities regard it as a way of sustaining the creation of infrastructure for public

---

1   For a presentation, see Cepremap, 'Well-Being Observatory', at cepremap.fr.

use without having to resort to debt. Thus, having undermined the public finances by organizing tax competition and requiring states to correct primary income inequalities, neoliberalism offers the public authorities a Pyrrhic solution. In accordance with often poorly negotiated clauses, the public actor is condemned to paying the private companies that own the infrastructure for many years into the future.

Even in the domain of research, the public authorities impose cooperation between the public and private sectors. Worse, credits for the former decline to the advantage of the latter, in the name of a greater 'efficiency' that is completely unproven. We find this, for example, in France with the Centre National de la Recherche Scientifique (CNRS), one of the world's leading public employers in basic research, which was incapable of paying maintenance annuities on the patents it owns, which it therefore abandoned by the hundred. Yet these patents are the outcome of research financed for decades by the French state.

Tax systems consistently encourage the creation of charities – foundations that operate as a substitute for the social, educational and even research activity of states.[1] Private actors thus become owners of what used to pertain to public decision-making and, fundamentally, democratic choice, while often undertaking communications operations.

If neoliberalism fuels propertarianism, the converse is also true. A market economy must maintain a minimum of equilibrium between customers and producers; and this assumes a minimum level of competition between private actors. Yet propertarianism erects barriers to the entry of new competitors. Whether it involves use of a patent or premises, starting up a business without property entails paying a rent. The ruptures induced by the new technologies – disruptions – are insufficient because they are too localized, and lead to the replacement of existing monopolists by

---

1   Gabrielle Fack and Camille Landais, *Charitable Giving and Tax Policy: A Historical and Comparative Perspective* (Oxford: Oxford University Press, 2016).

new monopolists. On the other hand, economic liberalism must help compensate for the monopolistic mechanics of property by relaxing regulatory constraints or encouraging entrepreneurs through the tax system.[1] In addition, enfeeblement of workers enables social dumping and thus facilitates the emergence of new competitors: labour market 'flexibility' – ease of dismissal or casualization – generates a flow of labour, while residential propertarianism tends to reduce voluntary labour mobility. Thus, the domination of property means that certain liberal policies on goods and services can stimulate activity.

The economically complementary relationship between propertarianism and neoliberalism cements the cohesions of conservative forces and their programme. It induces left-wing 'parties of government' to adhere to social liberalism, and the US Democratic Party to embrace a neoliberal progressivism. This economic dimension does not represent a direct challenge to liberal democracies; but propertarianism and neoliberalism contain the seeds of a rise of authoritarianism. Deregulation and the privatization of national enterprises and public services are reducing the role of the state to exclusively regalian domains. This circumscription automatically favours political offers promoting a state that is strong in its authority functions without threatening neoliberalism – quite the reverse, in fact. Having muzzled opposition forces, Viktor Orbán was able to make the transition from a pseudo-paternalist economic programme to an ultra-liberal programme affecting, in particular, labour contracts and conditions of pay.

Even when such a political offer does not attain power, an authoritarian drift can be observed, especially when the central state apparatus is historically powerful. Faced with a restriction of its prerogatives, such an apparatus can only retain its legitimacy by asserting its authority over citizens ever more firmly. The French case affords an illustration of this.

---

1   For a theoretical formalization of the complementarity between property rights and liberalism, see Philippe Aghion, Peter Howitt and Susanne Prantl, 'Patent Rights, Product Market Reforms and Innovation', *Journal of Economic Growth* 20: 3 (September 2015).

If, for an American liberal, Macron's France might seem like a haven, the reality is very different. Intermediate bodies (such as unions and even employers' organizations) are marginalized by the government. Resistance to the social or ecological order is met with increased repression and surveillance. The treatment of the 'yellow vests' movement is the most dramatic expression of this. This movement initially enjoyed broad popular approval. Senior officials in the Interior Ministry were concerned about the loyalty of their troops; they obtained from the government both premiums for the police and gendarmes deployed and considerable latitude to use force. The consequences are clearly described by a group of UN human rights experts: 'Since the start of the yellow vest protest movement in November 2018 … the restrictions on rights have resulted in a high number of arrests and detentions, searches and confiscations of demonstrators' possessions, and serious injuries have been caused by a disproportionate use of so-called "non-lethal" weapons like grenades and defensive bullets or "flashballs".'[1] At the same time, one-hundred doctors in public hospitals have condemned the central administration's 'placement on file' of hundreds of wounded yellow vests. Even peaceful resistance is to be suppressed. Thus, a few dozen symbolic removals of portraits of the head of state in public places by the non-violent action association COP21, in order to denounce the vacuum of his environmental policy, have given rise to spiralling repression by prosecutors (in France hierarchically linked to the justice minister, from whom they receive instructions), referral to the anti-trust office of the Gendarmerie, and dozens of activists being placed placed under detention, searched and sent before the courts.[2] The

---

1 United Nations Human Rights Council, 'France: UN Experts Denounce Severe Rights Restrictions on "Gilets Jaunes" Protesters', 14 February 2019, at ohchr.org. According to Agence France-Presse, by 4 April 2019 twenty-one men and two women (including high school students and even mere bystanders) had lost an eye after being shot in the head by a non-lethal weapon.

2 In one of the first judgements, delivered at the end of June 2019, the Strasbourg criminal court released three activists accused of conspiracy to steal. In March in Kolbsheim, a town on the route of a proposed bypass that

hardening of the state's attitude even affects press freedom. On 1 May 2019, 300 journalists protested: 'For three years now, we have witnessed a deliberate attempt to stop us from working, recording, and witnessing what happens during demonstrations.'[1]

Whether we broach it through the oldest aspect of the economy (land) or the most modern (knowledge), property and its capacity to capture rents are continuing to expand. This expansion is largely a political and legal construct; there is nothing natural about it. In addition, propertarianism and economic liberalism form a system. Exploiting economic changes, capital is armed to the teeth while accommodating the drift into authoritarianism.

---

aroused strong local opposition, these activists had, with the agreement of the mayor, taken down the portrait of the president. They then carried it to the worksite of the bypass before hanging it back up, undamaged, in the town hall.

  1   Opinion piece published on franceinfo.fr. It continues: 'There has not been a single demonstration or gathering in recent months without a journalist being attacked physically or verbally by the forces of order. More recently, a repressive course has been taken. Several colleagues have been questioned and detained for "participating in a group with a view to committing violence or damage", whereas we declare ourselves to be journalists.'

4

Winner Corporations

Capitalists are not the only ones to capture rents. Within the world of work, various social groups also grab significant slices of the cake.[1] Rather than sketching an exhaustive picture of this, a few well-chosen examples will facilitate a description of the mechanisms underlying their success. Does this success genuinely reflect their productivity and/or contribution to society? Beyond

---

1   A note on terminology: The distinction between capitalists and workers is not always absolute. Thus, self-employed workers who possess significant capital (an architect who owns her own office, for example) have an income that is realized from their labour and from this capital. Such income is therefore characterized as mixed: capital and labour. In practice, economists and national accounts employ conventions to separate labour income from capital income. Roughly speaking, there are two methods, which do not always yield the same results: the income from a self-employed person's labour is regarded as the same as that of an employee doing the same work, while income from capital is allocated based on the opportunity cost (rate of interest) of the business capital possessed by the self-employed person. I use the term 'social group' (not 'social category') deliberately. In sociology and social psychology, a social group is defined by common characteristics; shared goals and interests; an awareness, albeit vague, of belonging to this group; interactions that might even be merely potential. Within socio-professional categories, which are themselves a social construct (I shall return to this), groups coexist that vary in their ability to capture rents.

the phenomenon of the celebrity status of football players or CAC 40 bosses, how are we to explain the fact that some occupations and corporations manage to make themselves indispensable to the operation of the economy?[1] As we shall see, the concept of criticality is of decisive aid in understanding how some actors end up not just capturing rents, but rendering them legitimate.

Capital in Human Form

Numerically tiny groups end up capturing major rents: actors, sportspeople, designers, academics, and so on. They are sometimes characterized as stars. I will instead use the term 'capital-in-human-form' to refer to human beings who have become the financial or productive capital of the organizations that utilize them.[2] Although their nature assimilates them to capital, they remain in the category of 'labour' – whether in employment statistics or in the traditional measurement of income from work.[3]

European professional footballers offer the clearest illustration of human beings who have become capital. Every year, the football observatory of Neuchâtel University's Centre International d'Étude du Sport publishes the transfer value of football's stars. In summer 2017, the transfer values of Neymar and Kylian Mbappé to Paris Saint-Germain reached €222 million and €180 million, respectively. This is the value of a player qua financial capital of the club to which he is currently under contract. However,

---

1 The CAC 40 is a French stock-market index [Ed.].

2 Not to be confused with human capital, which (to adopt the definition used by the OECD) refers to 'the knowledge, skills, competencies and attributes embodied in individuals that facilitate the creation of personal, social and economic well-being'. B. Keeley, *Human Capital: How What You Know Shapes Your Life*, OECD Insights (Paris: Éditions OCDE, 2007), p. 29.

3 This is a question not of the technological complementarity between these agents and capital, but of their capitalist character. In addition, the individual is capital, not – as in the case of the intellectual property discussed in Chapter 2 – his production.

capital-in-human-form is not a slave: he retains the right of self-ownership, which guarantees him a return as a factor of production. Thus, Lionel Messi (Barcelona) is said to take home €35 million a year, and Neymar nearly €50 million.

Football is not the only sport to which this applies. Most professional sports teams (basketball, and so on), or major events within a single sport (tennis and tournaments, various athletic contests, and so on) are a sum of human-capital. Likewise, a blockbuster film requires its human-capital: a star director (by the director of the film '...'), a star screenplay writer, a star composer, star actors. Like capital, these human beings are subject to obsolescence, which is more rapid in the case of a sportsperson than an actor.

Obviously, this is nothing new. Fashion has always displayed its creators. And the big bosses who personify an enterprise and its strategy are likewise subject to this phenomenon of stardom, even if in their case other mechanisms predominate, to which I will return. But because these humans are similar in nature to capital, they benefit fully, as do their 'owners', from the mechanisms fostering them: globalization of markets, network effects, monopolistic rent, and protection of intangible property.

Let us return to the footballing example. The English Premier League enjoys exceptional broadcasting revenues. Not only is the English championship a key asset for the domestic operators who acquire it; it has become a global product bought by major TV subscription channels. In the years 2016–19, nearly £3 billion per annum were shared out among the clubs, depending on their ranking. To maintain this success, capital is required – in this case, players. Hence spectacular purchases took place, such as that in 2015 of Anthony Martial, a nineteen-year-old French player who was promising but without any real recommendation. Manchester United bought him from his 'owner' Monaco for €50 million, supplemented by three conditional bonuses of €10 million each (nomination for the Ballon d'Or prize, and so on). The principality's club would only receive 80 per cent of this sum: in 2013 it had bought Martial from Olympique Lyonnais, his formative club, for €5 million, with a profit-sharing deal of around 20 per cent on any future resale. For Olympique, training Martial was an investment in the literal sense.

To ensure receipt of a significant percentage of rents, players are collectively organized in professional unions confronting the clubs, their owners. Most of the national unions grouped together in the International Federation of Professional Footballers are powerful. In France, the Union Nationale des Footballeurs Professionnels claims more than 95 per cent membership among the thousand or more professionals. A strike can entail a complete cessation of activity, so that with each threat since the start of the century the English association (notably in 2001) and the French association (in 2008) have prevailed in their disputes.[1] Furthermore, teams' income, whether from merchandising or audiovisual revenue, depends on results – particularly access to the lucrative Champions League. These sporting results are generally correlated with the wage bill necessary to acquire the best players (whose individual performance is observable even if it is a team sport). If one adds the fact that owners have motives of prestige and influence in owning a club,[2] the bulk of the increase in rents in the European football industry – particularly audiovisual and merchandising rights – has been absorbed by the players' wage bill in the last decade.[3]

The North American context is different, with leagues of closed franchises where owners seek a return on their investment, regulation to ensure some form of sporting fairness – a salary cap (limit on the wage bill of the players for a team) or a draft (less highly-ranked teams have priority in recruiting new players) – and a share of audiovisual royalties. In the United States, partial or total

---

1   The Asociación de Futbolistas Españoles found things more difficult confronting the Spanish Liga. Its strike at the start of the 2011 season ended in a rapid agreement. By contrast, the strike of spring 2015 was declared illegal by the Spanish courts, enabling La Liga to carry on regardless.

2   On this point, see Luc Arrondel and Richard Duhautois, *L'argent du football* (Paris: CEPREMAP, 2018).

3   More precisely, the first decile that captures half of the total wage bill. See ibid.

strikes have peppered the major basketball, hockey and American football championships. At the same time, the clubs have no hesitation in resorting to lock-outs to force players to concede. Most collective bargaining agreements result in a balance in which the club owners retain a little over half the income.

Thus, on both sides of the Atlantic, the remuneration of sportspeople in leagues depends, on one hand, on the size of rents, which themselves derive from the monopolistic position of elite championships, and, on the other, on the relative bargaining power of owners and players. The art of creating a favourable balance of power, and defending a key position, is not confined to sportspeople: numerically much more significant social groups often know how to construct and exploit their *criticality*.

Criticality in the Service of Rents

Criticality is an idea present in various fields of engineering, but originally hails from nuclear engineering. The risk of criticality is the risk of a nuclear fission chain reaction. The Chernobyl disaster, like Fukushima's, was an accident of criticality. In the sphere of dependability, particularly of computer systems, criticality is defined as the probability of an accident multiplied by the gravity of its consequences:

$$\text{Criticality} = \text{probability} \times \text{gravity}$$

In other words, the greater the likelihood of a serious event occurring, the greater its criticality. Gravity can be measured in human, environmental or monetary terms. Step by step, I am going to extend this idea of criticality to an analysis of certain human groups within the organization of production.

Functional criticality

Let us take the example of an activity of security engineering: that of data. Summer 2015 was marked by the Ashley Madison saga. A subsidiary of the Canadian group Avid Life Media, Ashley Madison is an Internet-only player offering the service of extra-marital assignations. The network effect was in full swing in its development. According to its statements, 32 million people (mostly men), the majority of them in Anglophone countries, were registered on the site. It claimed, for example, to have 190,000 subscribers in Ottawa, out of a total population of 900,000! A group of hackers calling itself the Impact Team was able to enter the core of the company's systems and steal dozens of gigabytes of data on the site, including photographs, and the details of millions of clients and their sexual preferences. The latter were unveiled on the Internet in August 2015, with information that Ashley Madison claimed it had destroyed at the (paying) request of clients. The affair led to two suicides, including that of a priest, which shook the United States. Ultimately, the company was obliged to pay millions of dollars in damages to the victims of the hacking.

The criticality of data security for a company of this kind is equal to the probability of being the victim of hacking multiplied by estimated financial losses. In the case of Ashley Madison, the losses were the site's activity in its entirety plus the damages and interest paid to aggrieved customers. The probability of hacking is more difficult to assess, because it depends on parameters that are difficult to estimate – namely, the vulnerability of the technology and number of potential hackers. It is also bound up with the company's options as regards security. Theoretically, the optimizing enterprise will spend money on computer security personnel to a level where the marginal cost is equal to the marginal reduction of criticality (more precisely: its marginal expectation).

The more numerous and active the hackers, the greater the probability of hacking, and thus the greater the criticality of the security tasks. From a purely engineering perspective, criticality is essentially technological in origin – to which human error may be added as a parameter. The case of hacking shows that it also involves a construct within a social group. Computer engineers specializing in security and hackers often share the same training and skills, and encounter one another in the same social networks or large industry events. 'Repentant' hackers are regularly hired at high salaries onto security teams.

Without formal organization or intention, a global social group thus creates an increasing criticality. What happens next? The resources invested in security by businesses (or public authorities) have to expand. In short, the social group of security specialists and hackers captures an increasing share of the rents generated by network technologies.

At the same time, no tangible wealth-creation occurs: what is accomplished, rather, is the avoidance of destruction.[1] Worse, by mobilizing ever more investment and human capital in security, productive capacity may be impaired. Overall, labour productivity declines while the social group enjoys a growing share of income. It should be noted that this type of phenomenon is neglected by growth figures, which invariably overestimate the contribution of information technology.

The case of computer security pertains to a broader type of criticality that I shall characterize as functional. A role within an organization is critical to the extent it is perceived (or cultivates its perception) as necessary to the minimal functioning of the organization, or as capable of averting losses. Major enterprises can no longer do without marketers and communicators, whether internal or external; and the more an enterprise expands its marketing efforts, the greater is the perceived risk of eviction from the market among its competitors, who in their turn must therefore develop this role. In the sphere of finance, traders form a high-criticality social group.

It must be stressed that this criticality assumes a social dimension, whether that results from the behaviour of certain parts of the group (as in the case of hackers), or from certain information asymmetries. Let us take a commercial rail-transport company. Technologically, the presumably critical roles are those performed by railway workers (drivers, signal controllers, and so on).

---

1   However, if the end-user spends more on the security of her network, this service will be treated as value-added in the national accounts.

However, in the absence of powerful collective organization among these groups, it is roles like marketing and fare-optimization that are regarded by management as carrying the greatest criticality. The employees working in these occupations are at once socio-logically and physically closer to management, and hence in a position to prove that they are indispensable to the organization's 'value creation'.

Institutional criticality

Institutions supply a second source of criticality, which is often complementary to functional criticality. The regulatory environment forms part of the structuring of the economic system, productive organizations and society. The role of lawyer is necessary in any *Rechtsstaat*. But its degree of criticality for individuals and enterprises – namely, the estimated loss in the event of non-recourse to legal professionals – depends on the characteristics of national institutions.

Here a comparison between Britain and France is instructive. The two countries have the advantage of being fairly similar in terms of population size and structure.[1] Their levels of criminality are of the same order of magnitude, equivalent to what we find in the rest of western Europe but much lower than in the United States. According to data collected by Eurostat, the number of homicides recorded by the police in 2016 was 875 in mainland France and 879 in the UK.[2] The annual divorce rate is also similar: around 2.1 per cent per thousand inhabitants on both sides of the Channel, once again according to Eurostat figures. On the other hand, the two countries have very different conceptions of law. France has a codified legal system, whereas the UK relies on Common Law, which is essentially jurisprudential law. The idea here is not to discuss the comparative merits of these two legal systems, particularly as regards their economic efficiency;

---

1   Similar population pyramid, same proportion of youth or immigrants, a few more poor in the UK, a few more unemployed in France, and so on.

2   See ec.europa.eu.

it is simply a question of noting that, in the absence of a codified collection allowing each citizen – consumer, employee or entrepreneur – to access the essentials of the law, the British system compels recourse to legal specialists. It clearly enhances the criticality of juridical roles, especially those of barristers and associated professionals. What is the upshot for the number of professionals? London and Paris both contain concentrations of important international legal services, including law firms. A relevant comparison between the two countries requires us to look outside Paris and inner London. In addition, the boundaries of occupations are slightly different in the two countries, which necessitates some pooling. Outside Paris, adding up barristers, notaries, clerks and company lawyers, we arrive at a figure of around 60,000 in 2018.[1] Outside inner London, the number of solicitors[2] and barristers is nearly 100,000 – around 70 per cent more than in France.

'Classical' corporations

I have referred so far to social groups while ignoring their possible structuration. Social groups identifying with the same occupation or activity may be organized as a corporation with its own demands and interests, possibly enjoying certain privileges. Contemporary corporations in democratic market economies simply defend their own interests, no longer invoking a corporatist doctrine.[3]

---

1   Sources: INSEE for barristers, solicitors and clerks, and the Association Française des Juristes d'Entreprise for company lawyers.
2   Solicitors are responsible for tasks entrusted in France to certain barristers, notaries, clerks and company lawyers.
3   In antiquity, and then the Middle Ages, corporations existed in particular in artisanal occupations. They equipped themselves with defined statutes, a hierarchy, a policing system, rites, and even their own forms of devotion, and enjoyed a set of monopolies and privileges. The corporatist doctrine was inspired by this to propose an overview of the organization of society around institutional professional corporations represented in the state, which made decisions sanctioned by the state. Corporatism culminated in Europe in the fascist and collaborationist regimes as an anti-democratic alternative to

Regulated professions must not be confused with corporations. For legitimate reasons of public health or public order, many professions are regulated. This is true of most health professions. This regulation organizes the profession – for example, orders of doctors in each German *Land* – and often confers monopolies on it: for taxies, a *numerus clausus*, reserved spaces, exclusive rights to cruise. Regulated professions automatically possess a base from which to establish themselves as a corporation. However, on one hand, corporations exist outside these professions; on the other, a regulated profession is not always in a position to defend its interests.

Once again, a comparison between Britain and France, in this case relating to pharmacists, is useful in illustrating the degree of a regulated profession's capacity to capture rents. On account of European harmonization, the same level of training is required to enter the profession in both countries. Full mastery of the national language, however, is not strictly necessary. To practise, a pharmacist must be registered with the National Order of Pharmacists in France and the General Pharmaceutical Council in the United Kingdom.[1] The density of pharmacists in both countries lies at around the European average, with 84 pharmacists per 100,000 inhabitants in the United Kingdom, and as many as 105 in France, in 2015.[2] According to Eurostat data, both countries have more practising pharmacists than the more populous Germany.

---

liberalism and collectivism alike. Thus, in a speech of 1 May 1941, Pétain proclaimed: 'Abandoning all together the principle of the individual isolated in the face of the state and the practice of workers' and employers' coalitions ranged against one another, [the new corporatist order] establishes groups comprising all members of the same occupation: employers, technicians, workers. The centre of the group is therefore no longer social class, whether the employer's or the worker's, but the common interest of all those who are part of the same enterprise.'

1   Historically, the German model established in Alsace-Moselle served as a reference point for reflections in France in the 1930s, which were applied following the Liberation to replace Vichy's corporatist system.

2   Eurostat, 'Where to Go if You Want to Find a Pharmacist', 12 January 2018, at ec.europa.eu.

Britain and France also have in common the predominantly public financing of the health sector – through the National Health Service (NHS) in the UK and Assurance Maladie (health insurance) in France. In particular, while dispensaries are private enterprises, the prices of medicines prescribed and reimbursed (even if only partially) are regulated. The profit margins of community pharmacists on these products are likewise regulated. There are financial incentives for retail pharmacies to favour, for example, the use of generic medicines. Only non-reimbursed medicines and personal-care products have unregulated prices. In both countries, the state is also the main employer of hospital pharmacists.

However, the two countries diverge on one parameter: the spatial and capitalist regulation of retail pharmacies. British regulation has frequently been subject to significant reform, but two major principles persist: capitalist freedom to set up and to open. Freedom to establish a pharmacy strengthens competition between actors, but translates into pharmaceutical deserts.[1] British pharmacies can be owned by any type of actor as long as a pharmacist is present. Thus, independent dispensaries coexist with pharmacy chains where pharmacists are employees. Walgreens Boots Alliance is the most powerful chain (since the takeover of British Alliance Boots by US pharmacy giant Walgreens for £10 billion in 2014). With 2,500 sales points and 60,000 employees, it is ubiquitous in the country, including in large railway stations and airports; it boasts that 90 per cent of Britons are less than 10 minutes from a Boots. A Boots is typically a medium-sized or large shop with a section for dispensary for prescriptions and vast shelves of freely accessible medicines and personal-care products, and even a selection of foodstuffs. The dispensary is thus a loss leader; the margins on prescribed medicines are secondary to those realized on other products. Boots' business profits approach £1 billion in the United Kingdom.

---

1   See Maria Lluch and Panos Kanavos, 'Impact of Regulation of Community Pharmacies on Efficiency, Access and Equity. Evidence from the UK and Spain', *Health Policy* 95: 2 (2010).

The opening up of pharmacies' capital to corporate investors undermines the ability of British pharmacists to establish themselves as a corporation, and their capacity to capture rents is thus restricted. According to ONS statistics based on annual surveys of hours and earnings, the gross average remuneration of a British pharmacist has been around £37,000 since the start of the 2010s. In purchasing power parity (PPP) and net terms, this represents around €40,000 per annum.

French regulation of retail pharmacies is very different. In France, the opening of a new pharmacy in a commune is a matter of precise population criteria: it is not permitted in a commune of fewer than 2,500 inhabitants unless that commune previously had a pharmacy serving more than 2,500 inhabitants (for example, two towns of 1,500 residents each). If a pharmacy already exists in an area of more than 2,500 inhabitants, a second one may only be opened if the population exceeds 7,000 residents (and thereafter in increments of 4,500). The criteria are even stricter in Alsace-Moselle. The goal of the public health authorities is to distribute dispensaries across the country. Inevitably, however, this drastically reduces competition between retail pharmacies, thereby facilitating cooperation within the professional corporation. Ownership is also strictly supervised: the pharmacists must own the outlet of which they are the incumbents. The pharmacist who owns the pharmacy must practise her profession personally, and is not permitted to practise a different profession. She may only own or co-own a single pharmacy. Several associated pharmacists can form a company to run a pharmacy. Thus, the sector completely eludes national-level capitalistic actors.

The profession of pharmacists in France therefore finds itself dealing with Social Security and the state on its own. Corporatist associations of dispensaries negotiate directly with Assurance Maladie. In addition, the French pharmacist becomes, by design, a local notable with considerable capacity for influencing voters.[1]

---

1   This power explains the French government's abandonment in 2015 of its intention to open up the capital of pharmacies or relax the strict conditions

The General Inspectorate of Finances has estimated the net income of pharmacists in France for the year 2010.[1] Figures not challenged by the profession give net annual salaries for employees, and net income for the self-employed, of nearly €110,000 on average – about three times as much as in Great Britain. In macroeconomic terms, the additional rent captured by French pharmacists compared to their British colleagues is far from negligible, standing at around €5 billion. It should be noted that not all regulated professions in France, even in the medical sphere, are corporations. This is true, for example, of nurses. OECD data for 2015 suggest that a full-time French hospital nurse receives less than their British counterpart, with a wage just at the average income level (around €30,000 euros net per year).[2]

The comparison between nurses and pharmacists also allows us to exclude another argument habitually employed by the corporation of the latter in France: pharmacists supposedly receive remuneration far in excess of the rate abroad because the French assign greater importance to health in their preferences, as demonstrated in their high health expenditure. Were this true, the argument should apply to all health professionals, which is not the case. The huge pay gap between nurses and pharmacists reveals that we are far removed from a world where work is remunerated in accordance with some hypothetical natural productivity, or with levels of effort and skill.

Thus, depending on the parameters of regulation, a regulated occupation may or may not be able to become entrenched as a powerful corporation. They are not the only ones.

---

imposed on e-pharmacies. The socialist government already regarded the consumer law of 17 March 2014 as a victory, an act of authority in the face of pharmacists: it abolished the monopoly of pharmacies and opticians on the sale of cleaning products for lenses and their monopoly on the distribution of pregnancy tests.

1   Inspection Générale des Finances, *Les Professions réglementées*, report no. 2012 M057 03, 2013.

2   OECD, *Health at a Glance 2017* (Paris: OECD, 2017).

Poujadist corporations

An occupational body is not always in a position to inflict a significant loss on the economy by stopping work, other than in very localized fashion. Its criticality is therefore a priori low. However, it can enhance it by employing political intimidation or force to generate major potential losses. In this regard, we may refer to Poujadist corporations, even though they extend far beyond the borders of France.

Road-haulage companies and self-employed drivers are a striking example for Europe as a whole.[1] In acute competition with one another, they are nevertheless capable of mobilizing jointly to wrest subsidies or tax changes from the state. Tax changes and sudden hikes in diesel prices are the catalysts for their mobilization. They operate through high-criticality blockades, or even by resorting to wrecking. Companies may go so far as to require their employees to participate in these actions. Governments cave in almost systematically. Continent-wide, one of the largest mobilizations occurred in 2000. Faced with a rise in the price of diesel (around 40 per cent per annum), French truck drivers – joined by farmers, fishermen and even ambulance drivers – organized a blockade of oil refineries at the start of September, rapidly exposing the country to a fuel shortage. The French government immediately decided to open negotiations with the road-transport employers' federations. Buoyed by this success, the movement spread through Belgium, Germany, Italy and the Netherlands. It even extended to the UK. Truck drivers and farmers combined to blockade refineries, prompting panic buying and shortages. Having indicated that it would not concede, the Blair government decided to reduce taxation on 'clean' vehicles – the bulk of the lorry fleet. In its report, the Economic and Social Research Council estimated the minimum size of the tax concessions involved at £2 billion

---

1   By contrast, this is not the case in the United States. The last attempt at a blockade of Washington by self-employed truck drivers, in 2013, was a failure; only a few dozen trucks participated.

per annum.[1] While petrol prices continue to fluctuate, including downwards, these concessions are permanent.

'Self-referential' corporations

A final type of corporation has a much less visible mode of organization and action. It comprises professional bodies that, by dint of their position in private or public decision-making, are in a position to determine the modalities of their remuneration or criticality. They cannot be reduced to individual cases such as that of Nicolas Sarkozy who, once elected president of the French Republic in May 2007, immediately increased his pay by 170 per cent. The directors of large companies represent the archetype of a genuine corporation, which varies according to national or sectoral contours. Technically, their remuneration is a matter for the board of directors, an oversight committee, or a remuneration committee. But the emoluments of the members of these committees are themselves influenced by the CEO. There is massive endogamy: sitting on these bodies are other directors, shareholders' representatives or 'independent' figures.

On the pretext of prioritizing incentives, of attracting the best, pay tools proliferate: golden hellos, basic salaries, performance bonuses, stock options, golden parachutes, retirement packages.[2] To preserve a minimum of cohesion in their organization, but also to conceal their exceptional character, these benefits are extended to the totality of the enterprise's top executives. Ultimately, these tools do not even ensure that the director seeks to maximize the

---

1   Stephen Potter, Graham Parkhurst, Ben Lane, Barry Ubbels and Paul Peeters, *Taxation Futures for Sustainable Mobility: Final Report to the ESRC* (Milton Keynes: Open University, 2004).

2   Theoretically, the coupling is incoherent. If CEOs responded to financial incentives when their basic salary was already very high, their preference for risk should be enormous. However, they enjoy substantial golden parachutes that are supposed to protect them against the risk of losing their job – something that is compatible a priori only with a strong aversion to risk.

interest of the 'principal' (shareholders).[1] Such manipulation is even found in non-profit-making structures.[2]

In some countries, executives also know how to divert employers' organizations from their official objective – defending enterprise – to make them in addition sources of influence on public decisions affecting, for example, the individual taxation of executives. France affords a splendid example of this, with the misadventures of the wealth tax (*impôt de solidarité sur la fortune*) on fortunes of more than €1.3 million. Business assets were non-taxable, and various devices enabled most of those subject to the tax to evade it by investing in small and medium-sized enterprises. In fact, the wealth tax was highly favourable to enterprise. However, the two main employers' organizations – Medef and the CPME – kept up demands for its abolition, because their members were paying this tax on their non-business fortunes. Emmanuel Macron had it abolished in the first finance law of his five-year term; he has ruled out restoring it despite the resulting cost to the public finances, and the political cost highlighted by the yellow vests movement in late 2018.

Similarly, as Joseph Stiglitz has shown, US tax lawyers know how to manipulate the tax system to make it complex and open to influence, thereby rendering critical their role as tax experts for their corporate or private clients.[3] Financial lobbies also know how to press for regulations that enable them to take risks to win big while being retrospectively protected by the public authorities.

---

1   See, for example, Frédéric Palomino, *Comment faut-il payer les patrons?*, CEPREMAP booklet no. 21 (Paris: Presses de la Rue d'Ulm, 2011).

2   In France, the exorbitant remuneration of the directors of Sciences Po Paris, under the leadership of Richard Descoings, with the connivance of the board of directors of the Fondation Nationale des Sciences Politiques, was a sad example of this.

3   Joseph Stiglitz, *The Price of Inequality: How Today's Divided Society Endangers Our Future* (New York: W.W. Norton, 2013).

Attention to Working Conditions

It may be argued that, while certain social groups, including company executives, capture increasing rents, they also experience the pressures of increasingly stressful labour. This concern is central in numerous enterprises, where thought is given to how to improve the working environment of senior managers and 'creative experts', how to combine working and family life, and so forth. The stress suffered by managers and executives has become a journalistic cliché. It has led to the blossoming of new occupations, such as coaches for private individuals and enterprises.

This flowering might equally well reveal increased stress among these social groups, which tend to comprise graduates and males, or instead their ability to capture rents not only in the form of remuneration, but also of attention and efforts devoted towards their safety and working conditions. Which interpretation should we accept? To answer this question, let us turn to the sciences that study 'stress' at work.

Occupational psychology, in conjunction with numerous other disciplines including epidemiology, has developed a series of 'models' of stress – or, more generally, of psycho-social risk.[1] Two models in particular have demonstrated their relevance: those of Johannes Siegrist and Robert Karasek. These two models inform not only academic studies, but also action in private enterprises and public bodies.

Siegrist's model of effort–reward imbalance, developed since the late 1990s,[2] assigns a central place not only to factors relating to the person and personality at work, but also to their socio-economic context. As I noted in Chapter 1, the wage people are paid is perceived not simply in terms of its monetary value, but also as the value accorded to the work performed. More generally, approaches invoking the Siegrist model analyse the wage-labour

---

1   See, for example, Stavroula Leka and Aditya Jain, *Health Impact of Psychosocial Hazards at Work: An Overview* (World Health Organization, 2010).

2   Johannes Siegrist, 'Adverse Health-Effects of High-Effort/Low-Reward Conditions', *Journal of Occupational Health Psychology* 1: 1 (1996).

relationship as a contract of social reciprocity: to the efforts made at work there must correspond rewards in terms of wage, esteem, career prospects or job security. The multiplicity of parameters in such a contract of reciprocity creates 'contractual failures' that place people in a position of 'imbalance'. These imbalances may derive from excessive effort: physical, such as exposure to carcinogenic products or work intensity resulting in musculoskeletal problems; psychological, in response to orders that are contradictory or violate individual ethics (such as selling inappropriate products to vulnerable people); and social, when working hours are incompatible with family life. These imbalances also have their source in lesser rewards. The social groups of employees who see their pay increase, and their professional prospects maintained, would not be the ones most affected by stress.

Nevertheless, this analytical grid is imperfect. Let us take one of the neoclassical theories of wages – that of the wage as compensation: the wage compensates increased effort to ensure constant utility (compatible with a uniform relationship between wages and productivity). A more stressed manager would be 'compensated' (rather than rewarded) by a higher wage. In Siegrist's model, it would be concluded that, by virtue of this wage, he is no longer stressed – something that is open to doubt. Finally, transposing Siegrist's model to self-employed workers is problematic.

To get a firmer grip on this issue, we may now examine the Karasek founding model – named after an American sociologist – which has the advantage of focusing on work pressures and organization. Since this model has a long history, we possess retrospective data and an epidemiological literature confirming them and demonstrating health impacts.[1] These data have two

---

1   To facilitate this account, I have employed the original version of the model that appeared in the late 1970s. See the standard work by Robert Karasek and Töres Theorell, *Healthy Work: Stress, Productivity, and the Reconstruction of Working Life* (New York: Basic Books, 1990). Part of the literature completes the model with a third dimension: social support, including the help and recognition of colleagues and superiors. Conditions of remuneration do not form part of it. This additional dimension makes it possible to identify

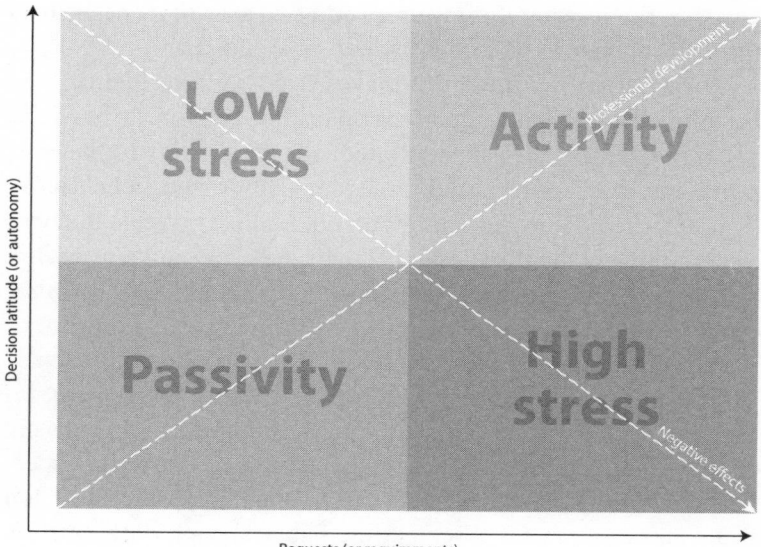

Figure 4.1 Karasek–Theorell Diagram

dimensions: on one hand, *demand* – resulting from the burden associated with the performance of tasks (defined by their accumulation in quantity, complexity and time pressures); on the other, *decision-making latitude* – the capacity to deploy one's skills (or to have skills adequate to the tasks demanded) and decision-making autonomy (organization of one's own work, working hours, influence on collective decisions, and so on).

Combining demand and latitude, we obtain four work situations: job strain – high demand and little decision-making latitude; activity – high demand but also great latitude; low tension; and passivity.[1] The Karasek–Theorell model makes it possible to

---

a particularly harmful cumulative situation – 'iso-strain' – which combines job strain and isolation, or an absence of social support. By definition, corporations and roles acknowledged as possessing high criticality are protected against these last factors.

1   Conventionally, the boundaries between high and low demands and decision-making latitudes are the median, or the mean, of workers' scores.

visualize them easily. To it we may add two axes that encapsulate the work done over several decades (see Figure 4.1).

A vast scientific literature makes it possible to identify the harmful effects of work situations on health. Their positive effects are less scientifically substantiated: the diagram's south-west/ north-east diagonal indicates professional flourishing when activity is enriched. However, studies do not make it possible to give a clear ranking of the situations of activity, passivity and low tension in terms of multidimensional impacts on health. On the other hand, aetiological studies converge in showing that exposure to job strain very significantly increases the risks of cardiovascular pathologies and mental health problems.[1] These results remain statistically significant even when taking account of factors partially endogenous to job strain (for cardiovascular risk: arterial hypertension, hyper-cholesterolaemia, over-weight, and smoking). Job strain also exacerbates absenteeism, diabetes, poor work satisfaction, and other general health indicators.[2]

Studies conducted in numerous OECD countries disclose a marked social gradient. In short, managers and intellectual professionals evince a much lower prevalence of exposure to job strain than other workers. A partial corollary of this social gradient is that many more women are in a situation of job strain. Drawing on massive European surveys of working conditions, the work commissioned and carried out by the European Foundation for the Improvement of Living and Working Conditions in Dublin confirms on a continental scale that the situation of managers is

1   See, for example, Mika Kivimäki, Marianna Virtanen, Marko Elovainio and Anne Kouvonen, 'Work Stress in the Etiology of Coronary Heart Disease – A Meta-Analysis', *Scandinavian Journal of Work and Environmental Health* 32: 6 (2006); and the report by the French committee of experts, *Mesurer les facteurs psychosociaux de risque au travail pour les maîtriser* (2011) – pdf available at travail-emploi.gouv.fr.

2   Isabelle Niedhamer, Jean-François Chastang and Simone David, 'Importance of Psychosocial Work Factors on General Health Outcomes in the National French SUMER Survey', *Occupational Medicine* 58: 1 (2008).

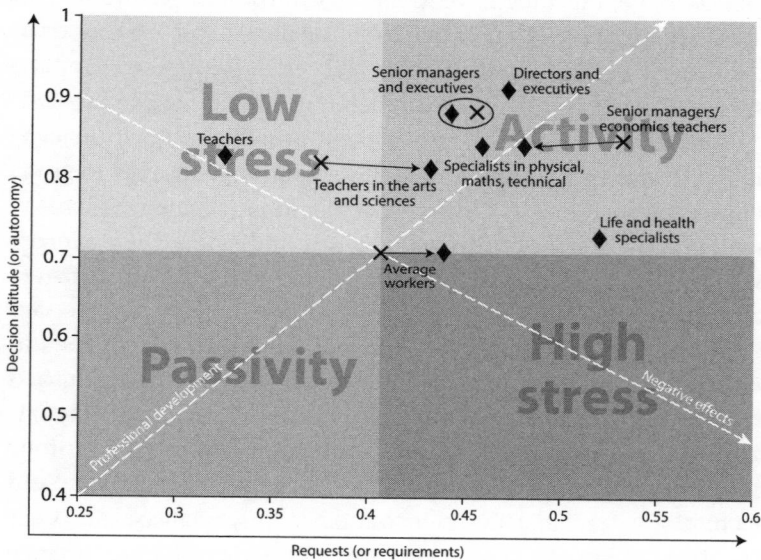

Figure 4.2 'Higher' Occupations in the Fifteen-Member EU (UK Included) in a Karasek–Theorell Diagram (comparison between 1995 and 2015)

Source: Author's calculations from European surveys of working conditions.

Field: Observations weighted so as to be representative of the totality of workers in the fifteen-member EU. Karasek's approaches are basically confirmed in the case of employees. The exclusion of the self-employed only marginally alters the results for the fifteen-member EU.

Definitions: Demand is defined by a score comprising two questions: 'Does your job involve working at very high speed?' and 'Does your job involve working to tight deadlines?' The answers range from 'never/almost never' to 'almost all of the time/all of the time'. Decision-making latitude is assessed on the basis of a score aggregated from three binary questions: 'Are you able to choose or change your order of tasks?', 'your methods of work?', 'your speed or rate of work?'. The scores are standardized from 0 to 1.

Key: The average scores by occupation are represented: ♦ = 2015; × = 1995.

The arrows designate the changes for an occupation between 1995 and 2015, except for senior managers and executives, for which the average scores are surrounded by an oval. The occupations correspond to the international categorization ISCO-88.

far removed from job strain.[1] Certainly, their work demands are considerable, but they have great decision-making latitude, and are therefore most often in 'activity'. The initial 2015–16 rounds of the American Working Conditions Survey, based on the European survey, suggest comparable results in the United States.[2]

The European surveys also make it possible to track the evolution of work situations by major occupation from 1995 to 2015.[3] Figure 4.2 positions the 'higher' occupations and the whole set of workers in a Karasek–Theorell diagram indicating their average scores. The two major 'higher' groups are senior managers and intellectual and scientific professionals.[4] The first category essentially comprises public- and private-sector managers and executives; within the private sector, directors can be distinguished from executives in 2015.[5] Intellectual and scientific professionals are more diverse. In 2015, they could be distributed into four sub-groups: specialists in the physical sciences, mathematics and technology; teachers; life-science and health specialists; and 'other specialists'.[6] Finally, senior executives and specialists in finance can be identified.

---

1   Chaira Ardito, Roberto Leombruni, Lia Pacelli and Angelo d'Errico, *Health and Well-Being at Work: A Report Based on the Fifth European Working Conditions Survey* (Dublin: Eurofound, 2012).

2   See, for example, Nicole Maestas, Kathleen J. Mullen, David Powell, Till von Wachter and Jeffrey B. Wenger, 'The Value of Working Conditions in the United States and Implications for the Structure of Wages', IZA DP no. 11925 (2018).

3   The data are available for non-commercial use in UK data archives. Eurofound has constructed sectoral and occupational variables that correct some discontinuities in nomenclature.

4   The so-called ISCO-1 and 2 classes. The classification of occupations in these international surveys corresponds to international norms that may differ from the classifications used nationally, such as socio-professional categories in France. The norm used here is called ISCO (International Standard Classification of Occupations) 1988.

5   They run a business or organization containing at least three executives.

6   The specialists in physical sciences, mathematics and technology notably contain engineers, researchers in these disciplines, computer scientists and architects. Teachers are of all levels, from primary to tertiary. Life-science

None of these 'higher' occupations is situated as average on the 'job strain' scale in 2015. With the exception of teachers, all of them appear in the 'activity' frame. However, health and life-science specialists are on average closest to job strain, and one-third of them are on this scale for 2015. By contrast, the other profession-als – particularly senior managers – are very far removed from it. This does not mean that none of them experiences job strain – one in seven did so in 2015 – but that, on average, the occupation is spared from it. Executive managers, managers and finance specialists certainly experience high job demands. But they also benefit from very considerable autonomy, placing them on the axis where professional development is most immediately evident.

Did their work situation deteriorate in the Union between 1995 and 2015? In line with a wide body of science, we can observe a phenomenon of work intensification in the case of all workers: demands increased while decision-making latitude did not.[1] However, senior managers appear to escape this dynamic, their average scores remaining virtually unchanged. Intellectual and scientific occupations – once again, highly diverse – have passed from 'low tension' to 'activity', with an increase in demands upon them but a maintenance of autonomy. More specifically, the occu-pations of senior manager and finance specialist have benefited from a reduction in job demands.

In short, even abandoning the Siegrist model, which assigns considerable importance to professional recognition (including wages), it is difficult to conclude that senior managers – the elites of the financial sector – are increasingly exposed to stress; they are even somewhat protected from it. These results corroborate an interpretation that regards the attention paid to executive stress as evidence not of an epidemic but, on the contrary, of executives' ability to wrest advantages from the system.

---

and health specialists range from nursing managers via pharmacists to doctors. Other specialists are even more diverse: artists, writers, barristers, bishops, human and social science researchers.

1   See Philippe Askenazy, *Les Désordres du travail* (Paris: Éditions du Seuil, 2004).

Overall, then, social groups organized as a corporation and/or possessing a criticality perceived as high are in a position to enjoy or construct significant situational rents. The point here is not to denounce these groups. It is, in the first instance, theoretical in kind. The aim of Chapter 3 was to demonstrate that capitalistic rents are not a natural or technological remuneration of capital, but the result of propertarianism. A similar observation is in order for the social groups that turn out to be the winners: their remuneration and the attention paid to their working conditions are very far removed from their marginal productivity. They are basically a social and institutional construct.

5

'Less-Skilled' Effort

Analyses of job polarization proliferate today, in sociology as well as economics.[1] What is it? When we consider the occupational hierarchy in accordance with initial pay levels, we note that, in OECD countries – especially the United States – that employment has increased in two categories of occupation over the long term: the best-paid and the least well-paid. At the same time, the share of occupations on intermediate pay (around the median) is shrinking. The latter, regarded as the base of the middle class, are said to be the victim of de-industrialization and globalization, and are being replaced in the routine tasks they once performed by technology. Consequently, labour's share in value-added is declining in proportion to its replacement by machines. For their part, the 'low skilled' are said to be in greater demand.[2] In addition to

---

1   Among the very large number of works on the subject, see Daron Acemoğlu and David H. Autor, 'Skills, Tasks and Technologies: Implications for Employment and Earnings', in Orley Ashenfelter and David E. Card, eds, *Handbook of Labor Economics, Vol. 4* (Amsterdam: Elsevier, 2011).

2   Throughout the text, the terms 'low', 'un-' and 'less skilled' will appear in inverted commas. These terms, widely used but no less pejorative for that, structure debates on occupations when they are in fact based on changing conventions. Many specialists in job polarization, for example, define *unskilled* occupations as those historically paid least.

increasing social needs (fuelled, for example, by dependency in old age), a new trickle-down is said to be occurring: the wealthiest 1 per cent – and, more generally, the most highly skilled – increasingly consume personal services. But workers in the latter are largely unproductive and, above all, have no prospect of increasing their productivity. Unproductive, they 'naturally' merit pay that is, at best, stagnant. Let us see if these allocations of income are robust.

Intensification and Burn-Out

At the end of Chapter 4, we saw that senior management in Europe has not experienced both an increase in demands at work and a loss of autonomy. For their part, other occupations have developed along the axis of deleterious work situations, as shown in Figure 5.1, which reproduces the Karasek–Theorell diagram. Practically all of them, from intermediate occupations to so-called elementary occupations, were the victims between 1995 and 2015 of increasing demands without a palpable improvement in decision-making latitude – or, worse, with a decline in autonomy. On average, so-called 'unskilled' workers and employees (cleaners, refuse collectors, and so on) did not lose autonomy. However, their autonomy was limited from the outset, and, more importantly, their workload increased. In 2015, those such as service personnel and sales assistants found themselves in a situation of job strain. The outcome is the same, based on a Siegrist-style approach, since these workers often experience a lack of recognition of their work, and even a decline in wage recognition.

A worker aged around forty in 2019 is liable to have experienced no regime other than an intensification of work. And intensification over several years, even decades, ultimately translates into burn-out: irreversible damage to the physical and cognitive spheres reduces productive capacity, the ability to sustain work, and employability. In addition, many workers face multiple forms of exposure: carcinogenic products, repro-toxic substances and

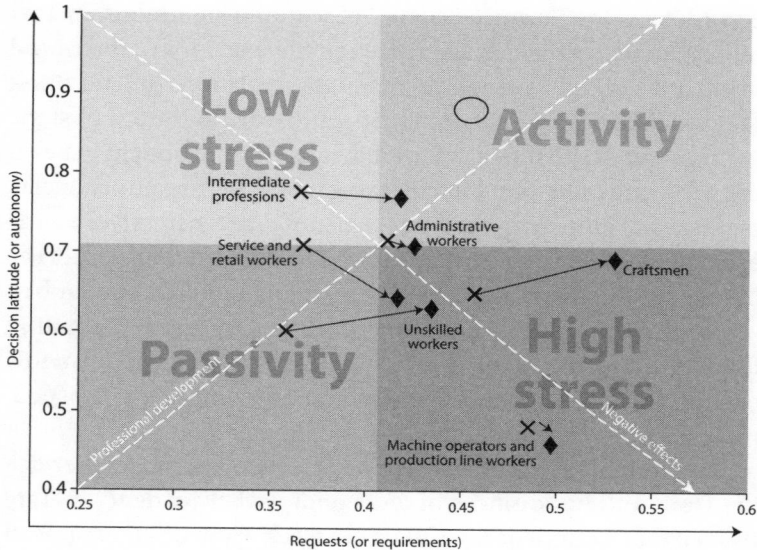

Figure 5.1 'Less-Skilled' Occupations in the Fifteen-Member EU (UK Included) in a Karasek–Theorell Diagram (comparison between 1995 and 2015)

Source, definition, field: see Figure 4.2 (Chapter 4).

Key: The average scores by occupation are represented. ♦ = 2015, × = 1995.
The arrows indicate the changes for an occupation between 1995 and 2015.
The oval recalls the position of senior managers and directors in 1995 and 2015.
The occupations correspond to the international categorization ISCO-88.

mutagens, fine particles, and so on.[1] In this respect, there are several disturbing indicators: healthy life expectancy is no longer increasing in Europe; only life expectancy with limitations is continuing to rise.[2] Women seem to be particularly affected. Thus,

---

1   Interested readers may refer to the results of the remarkable French SUMER surveys. The Surveillance Médicale des Risques employs a network of occupational doctors to complete questionnaires during mandatory medical visits, offering a precise picture of individual exposure. See 'Des risques professionnels contrastés selon les métiers', *Dares analyses* 39 (May 2014) – pdf available at travail-emploi.gouv.fr.

2   A notion developed in demography and epidemiology, healthy life expectancy, is obtained by breaking down life expectancy into two life

according to the European survey of working conditions, in 2015 more than half of women aged between fifty and fifty-four engaged in what are called 'low-skilled' manual occupations did not think they would be capable of doing the same work at the age of sixty.

These work situations, which might have been thought to be on the wane, are even found in emerging jobs. Large-scale producers of waste and greenhouse gas, our societies grant themselves a clear ecological conscience – without an ecological consciousness of the human! For example, our selective recycling requires a new job of inspection and manual correction of our sorting errors. Operating the length of conveyor belts in vast factories, workers perform this backbreaking job without the slightest autonomy; it is isolated, prescribed, physically demanding and dangerous.

In addition, atypical working hours are increasing to service the front and back offices of an economy that tends to operate twenty-four hours a day, seven days a week. Concern is expressed for traders and senior managers who cannot switch off. But here, too, a little economic and social tourism would be highly instructive. During the working week in London, from 5 p.m. the pubs fill up, with commingling lawyers and financiers. The offices of the City, La Défense, Lower Manhattan, and even Shinjuku and Gangnam, are emptied of their executives at weekends. They are to be found with the capitalist elite and its offspring in coastal or ski resorts, golf clubs or the stands (even during the week) of Wimbledon, Flushing Meadows, Roland-Garros and Melbourne.

At the same time, the opening hours of shops, especially food retailers, extend to the weekend, and towards late evening. Even if we accept the fiction that the front-office employees engaged in such activities – checkout operators, and so on – are volunteers,

---

expectancies, with and without activity limitations. For this purpose, the prevalence of activity limitations observed in the general population is introduced into the calculation of life expectancy. In Europe, the requisite data derive from the annual EU-SILC survey coordinated by Eurostat for the whole European Union (but also Switzerland, Israel and Iceland). See the European Health and Life Expectancy website, at eurohex.eu.

these extended schedules compel the back-office personnel who come in after closure, for maintenance and administrative work, to work hours that are increasingly disorientating socially. Through a knock-on effect, public transport must also extend its hours (train and tram drivers, security personnel, and so on). Those working in densely populated areas are especially affected. Since senior management maintains its working hours, temporal inequalities deepen. A fascinating survey conducted in US hospitals by American sociologists shows clearly how inequalities have risen between doctors who possess margins of autonomy over their choice of worked hours and female nursing auxiliaries who are subject to imposed work schedules with very severe financial penalties in the event of absence.[1]

Along with changes in working hours and time, work intensification is the result of a resurgent productivism over the last quarter-century.[2] Behind the terms 'lean production', 'just-in-time', 'high-performance practices', and 'quality norms' has taken root a logic of exploitation of the totality of human capacities, physical and mental alike. Various technologies are employed to stipulate the work of a high proportion of the 'less skilled', while multiplying the objectives they must meet.

In fact, while the machine may replace the human, above all it transforms the tasks the human must perform, reshuffling job allocation in the workplace. In the industrial domain, those performing quality control – an 'intermediate' job – see their tasks transferred to the productive level. Quality control is carried out by each worker, whose cognitive capacities had hitherto not been fully utilized. This new task requires a learning process and a degree of skill. Even so, the worker will not change occupational category, whether in the job statistics or the classifications constructed by the collective conventions of the countries or sectors that make use of them.

---

1   Dan Clawson and Naomi Gerstel, *Unequal Time: Gender, Class, and Family in Employment Schedules* (New York: Russell Sage Foundation, 2015).

2   See Philippe Askenazy, *Les Désordres du travail* (Paris: Éditions du Seuil, 2004).

In the case of services, large food retailers – the largest private employers in the advanced countries – afford an illustration of these mutations. Cashiers now only occasionally have to tap in prices manually; but they are subject to acceleration in the pace of product scanning. A cashier can handle two tons of products in a day, and their activity is completely open to inspection thanks to technology. Lists of the most productive can be found in staffrooms; some shops even devise weekly competitions, with prizes to be won. At the same time, cashiers face an accumulation of mental tasks – multiplicity of means of payment, loyalty cards, monitoring of customers to prevent 'shrinkage' – while responding to the contradictory injunction to satisfy customers by humouring them.[1] In small and medium-sized shops, multitasking is required (moving from operating the till to stacking shelves). Even the development of automatic tills does not abolish the human: standing, the cashier becomes a till assistant. Contrary to the cliché holding that digital technology ensures an interface between humans, it is the assistants who create the interface between customer and machine. The machine can neither debug itself nor monitor scammers – or the merely careless – and still less help customers who are in a hurry. Cashier, till assistant: the terminology of human resources has been enriched to show these workers that the world of business recognizes them. But the recognition stops there. Despite even more pronounced multitasking, and the deployment of new tasks and skills, these jobs have not been reclassified: they remain 'unskilled', with pay to match.

Let us stick with retail. In the first instance, floor managers were liberated from stock management, which has been routinized by the use of bar codes. This made it possible to add to their role advising customers and organizing teams, as well as manual tasks such as a share of the shelf-stacking, where the number of items has proliferated. Outside large shops, the next step was the abolition of the hierarchical level of floor manager. But the tasks of organizing and advising have not disappeared; they are performed

---

1   'Shrinkage' is a euphemism for theft.

Table 5.1 Average Level of Skills Deployed by Occupation in the OECD in 2011–12

	Learning at work	Co-operative skills	Physical skills	Reading	Numeracy
Elementary occupations	1.6	2.3	3.4	1.0	1.4
Plant and machine operators, and assemblers	1.7	2.3	3.0	1.4	1.7
Craft and related trades workers	2.0	2.7	3.4	1.7	1.6
Service and sales workers	2.0	2.6	2.7	1.7	1.8
Clerical support workers	1.9	2.2	1.1	2.1	2.1
Technicians and associate professionals	2.1	2.4	1.4	2.3	2.2
Professionals	2.2	2.2	1.0	2.6	2.2
Managers	2.1	2.6	1.2	2.7	2.6

Source: OECD, OECD Skills Outlook 2013, Chapter 4.

Field: Twenty members of the OECD, including the United States, France, Germany, England and Northern Ireland.

Key: Skills are measured through a series of questions:

• Cooperative skills: 'What proportion of your time do you usually spend co-operating or collaborating with co-workers?'

• Physical aptitudes: 'How often does your job usually involve working physically for a long period?'

For these variables, the use of skills ranges from 0 to 4: 0 indicates the lack of utilization of the skill; 1 its utilization less than once a month; 2 less than once a week, but at least once a month; 3 at least once a week but not daily; and 4 daily utilization.

The other variables are derived from the answers to several questions.

by first-level employees, who often remain classified among elementary occupations.

A glance at the skills deployed at work indicates the differences and similarities between occupations. The OECD carried out a vast survey in 2011–12, designed to measure the reading and numeracy skills of adults (aged from sixteen to sixty-five) and then construct skill scales.[1] Table 5.1 groups these skill scores by major occupation. A predicable hierarchy may be noted for numeracy, reading and physical aptitude. By contrast, learning skills (learning from supervisors or colleagues; learning on the job; remaining up to date with new products and services) indicate a hierarchy, but the divergences are not so pronounced. Meanwhile, in the skill of cooperating with colleagues, the 'higher' occupations perform no better than the 'less skilled'.

The Increasingly Well-Qualified 'Less Skilled'

Work transfer and learning in a professional context proceed all the more smoothly because the 'less skilled' are increasingly well-qualified, and hence in a position to perform them efficiently. The phenomenon is particularly clear in Europe over the last two decades. Eurostat's Labour Force Survey makes it possible to track the level of diploma by occupation from 1996 to 2014. On account of changes in classification between the two dates, we can only track aggregate levels of degrees and occupations in accordance with international classifications (ISCED-11 and ISCO-08). Table 5.2 shows that educational levels have risen systematically. Thus, administrative employees now have degrees similar to those held in intermediate occupations (technicians, sales representatives, nurses, and so on) twenty years earlier. Women in jobs delivering direct services to private individuals and sales (hairdressers,

---

1   See OECD, *OECD Skills Outlook 2013: First Results from the Survey of Adult Skills* (Paris: Éditions OCDE, 2013). Unfortunately, the second phase of the survey involved only nine countries.

Table 5.2 Level of Diploma of Persons in Employment in the Fifteen-Member European Union in 1996 and 2014 for 'Less-Skilled' Occupations (as a percentage)

	1996			2014		
	Primary or less	Secondary	Tertiary	Primary or less	Secondary	Tertiary
Elementary occupations: Men	67	29	4	49	44	7
Elementary occupations: Women	74	24	2	51	42	7
Plant and machine operators, and assemblers	59	38	3	40	53	7
Craft and related trades workers	46	48	6	32	59	9
Service and sales workers: Men	49	43	8	28	55	16
Service and sales workers: Women	48	46	6	26	59	15
Clerical support workers	29	58	12	14	60	26

Source: Author's calculations from Eurostat's European Labour Force Survey.

Key: In 1996, 29 per cent of men in an elementary occupation had secondary-school qualifications; in 2014 the figure was 44 per cent.

waitresses, and so on) have the same educational level as administrative employees in the mid 1990s.

This development is often construed as evidence of downgrading.[1] It is true, according to the PIAAC 2011–12 survey, that up to

---

1   For example, this thesis has become commonplace (and is widely criticized) in French debates, challenging the process of educational democratization implemented by François Mitterrand from the 1980s. See Louis Chauvel, *Les Classes moyennes à la dérive* (Paris: Éditions du Seuil, 2006), and

one-third of Japanese and French workers consider themselves 'overqualified' for their job. On this interpretation, the rise in educational levels in some occupations is the result not of demand on the part of businesses, but of an excess of graduates who are obliged to accept unskilled jobs. If we retain a fixed view of occupations as they might have been characterized decades ago, it does indeed seem incongruous that, in contemporary Europe, one employee in six in direct personal services and sales holds a university degree. But such reasoning is absurd, because, under a title assigned twenty or thirty years ago, a job or occupation makes very different demands today. Indeed, the public policy developed in favour of educational democratization can be analysed as a response to the growing needs of businesses and states that are themselves employers. Finally, the sense of downgrading is an inevitable consequence of the non-recognition of skills,[1] particularly when it comes to wages.

In reality, educational democratization in Europe has made it possible to catch up with the United States, where qualification levels used to be much higher. The educational structure of the US population being relatively stable, a glance at the United States offers an indication of the level of diploma expected. In addition, changes in organization, technology and employment in

---

Éric Maurin, *La Peur du déclassement. Une sociologie des récessions* (Paris: Éditions du Seuil, 2009).

1   OECD, *OECD Skills Outlook 2013* engaged in a problematic but nevertheless suggestive exercise. The PIAAC survey proceeded to test the reading and numeracy skills of the people questioned. On the basis of this individual information, the OECD looked to see whether people who declared themselves 'overqualified' did better in the tests than the 95 per cent of workers in the same occupation in the same country who stated they possessed the skills required for their job. The percentage of those overqualified in reading and/or numeracy hovered around the 6 per cent mark in France, and between 8 and 10 per cent in Japan, as in the United States. This is at once significant and a low figure, given the 31 per cent of Japanese and French people who consider themselves too highly qualified for their post. The main limitation of this analysis is that it is based on an aggregate classification of occupations, when we have seen that such a level masks significant diversity.

Table 5.3 Educational Level of Persons Aged over Twenty-Five in Employment in Selected Occupations in the United States (2016–17, as a percentage)

	Less than high school diploma	High school diploma or equivalent	Some college, no degree	Associate degree	Bachelor degree or more
Home health aides	12.7	36.2	31.9	10.0	9.1
Security guards	6.2	34.1	32.6	9.9	17.3
First-line supervisors of food preparation and serving workers	12.2	35.0	28.9	10.2	13.8
Cook (except chef)	29.4	40.9	18.4	5.5	5.8
Waiters and waitresses	12.6	32.0	30.4	9.3	15.6
Janitors and cleaners, except maids and housekeeping cleaners	24.9	43.7	19.2	5.9	6.1
Hairdressers, hairstylists, and cosmetologists	6.2	44.2	31.5	11.1	6.9
Concierges	11.1	28.3	28.1	11.0	21.4
Tour and travel guides	4.0	18.1	26.2	7.3	44.5
Fitness trainers and aerobics instructors	2.6	14.6	24.2	10.1	48.5
Cashiers	15.5	40.5	24.7	7.4	11.8
Retail salespersons	6.9	29.1	27.6	10.2	26.3
Telemarketers	5.8	29.7	31.1	11.5	21.8
Receptionists and information clerks	5.3	31.1	32.3	11.2	20.0
Plumbers	16.1	46.4	25.0	7.3	5.2
Automotive glass installers and repairers	15.2	55.5	24.4	2.6	2.4
Subway and streetcar operators	8.7	34.7	29.8	13.9	12.8

Source: Bureau of Labor Statistics, Employment Projections Program, on the basis of the American Community Survey (2016 and 2017).

the United States often foreshadow those that will be experienced by European economies (and even advanced Asian ones). The US Bureau of Labor Statistics has drawn up a table of educational levels by occupation for those aged over twenty-five (thus avoiding student-worker effects) for the years 2016 and 2017. Table 5.3 provides some examples of it in personal, transport and repair services. Thus, we observe that occupations regularly classified in the unskilled or low-skilled categories contain significant percentages of university graduates: one-half of auxiliary nurses, whose medical responsibility is increasing, have gone through university; one-quarter of concierges and receptionists have a diploma marking two years of higher education. On the other hand, occupations largely untouched by task transfer but affected by an intensification of work, such as cooks, still mainly include those with secondary qualifications or below.

From the Usefulness of the Middle Class to That of Polarization

Taking account of workers' educational level also makes it possible to look again at the polarization of the world of work since at least the start of the 1990s. The idea of polarization induced by technological changes is often attributed to a US economist, David Autor, in a work that appeared at the turn of the millennium. Yet the idea long predates this. It emerged fifteen years earlier, essentially in US trade-union circles. The titles of the reports by the Industrial Union Department of the AFL-CIO – *Are Middle Level Jobs Disappearing?* (1983) and *The Polarization of America* (1986) – are explicit.[1] They contain most of the current arguments. In 1985, Neal Rosenthal collated them, characterizing them as the 'fears' of proponents of an end to the middle class: decline of employment in the industries of the second industrial revolution; rapid growth

---

1   Lucy S. Gordon, *Are Middle Level Jobs Disappearing?* (Washington: AFL-CIO, 1983); Owen Bieber, *The Polarization of America: The Loss of Good Jobs, Falling Incomes and Rising Inequality* (Washington: AFL-CIO, 1986).

of high-tech industries with bipolar employment structures; and strong growth in employment in badly paid service occupations.[1] But the head of the forecasting division of the Bureau of Labor Statistics sought to dismantle these arguments by unpacking the data of his services, concluding that 'given BLS projections of employment by occupation, bipolarization is not likely to occur between 1982 and 1995'.

In 1980s America, the notion of the 'great American middle class' – a vast, growing middle class encompassing citizens with similar incomes and shared values – remained extremely useful. The major compression of wage inequalities from the end of the Second World War until the 1970s was a reality that made it possible to reject the relevance of any analysis of US society in terms of class struggle. The Reaganite theory of trickle-down from the wealthiest to the rest of society complemented the vision of a shared lot.

Following the fall of the Berlin Wall, capitalism no longer needs the concept of a dominant middle class. On the contrary, the concept of polarization has become, as we have seen, a lever for naturalizing inequalities. It makes it possible to justify neoliberal labour market policies intended to demolish the 'rigidities' that impede job creation at the bottom end of the wage scale.

Far removed from a conflictual social vision, the 'neutral' approach to classes by income – which can be linked to the Chicago School and, prior to it, to Weber – is deployed in economics and sociology alike to demonstrate job polarization. An alternative approach can be developed that is just as 'neutral'. The first study to have done so, in 2017, was conducted by the European Job Monitor of the European Foundation for the Improvement of Living and Working Conditions. It involves constructing an occupational hierarchy based on workers' observed educational level.

Figures 5.2a and 5.2b show the changes in employment in the European Union at the height of the Great Recession between 2008

---

1   Neal Rosenthal, 'The Shrinking Middle Class: Myth or Reality?', *Monthly Labor Review*, March 1985.

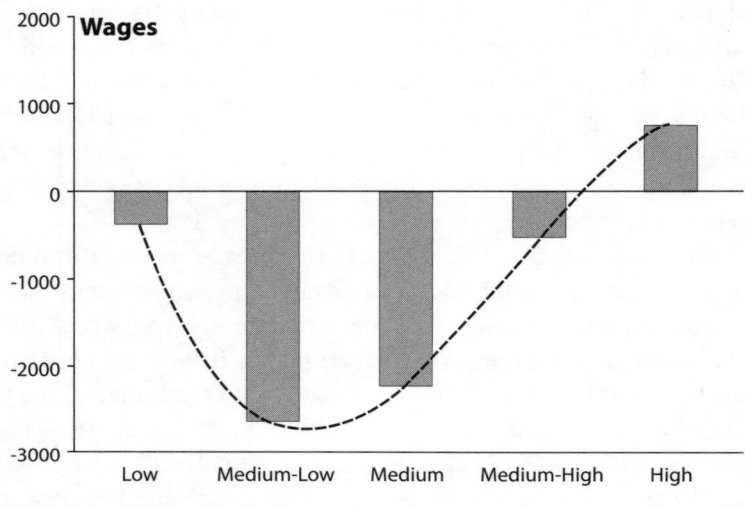

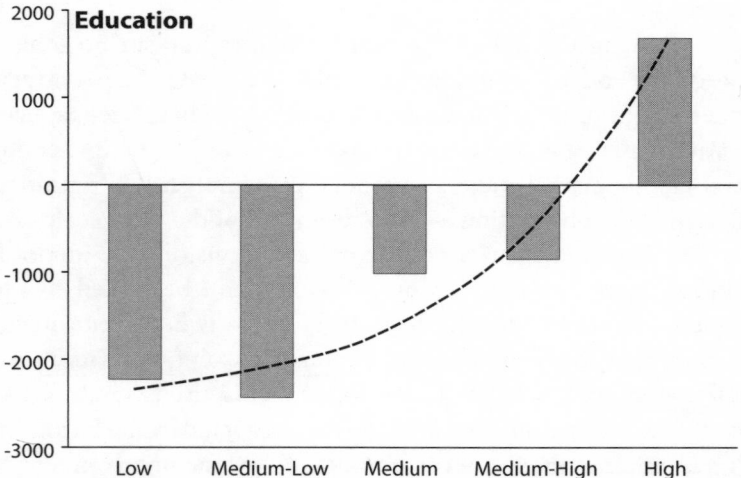

Figure 5.2a Net Job Creation or Destruction (in Thousands) in the (pre-Brexit) European Union 2008–10 in 5 Quintiles of Occupations Ranked by Wages

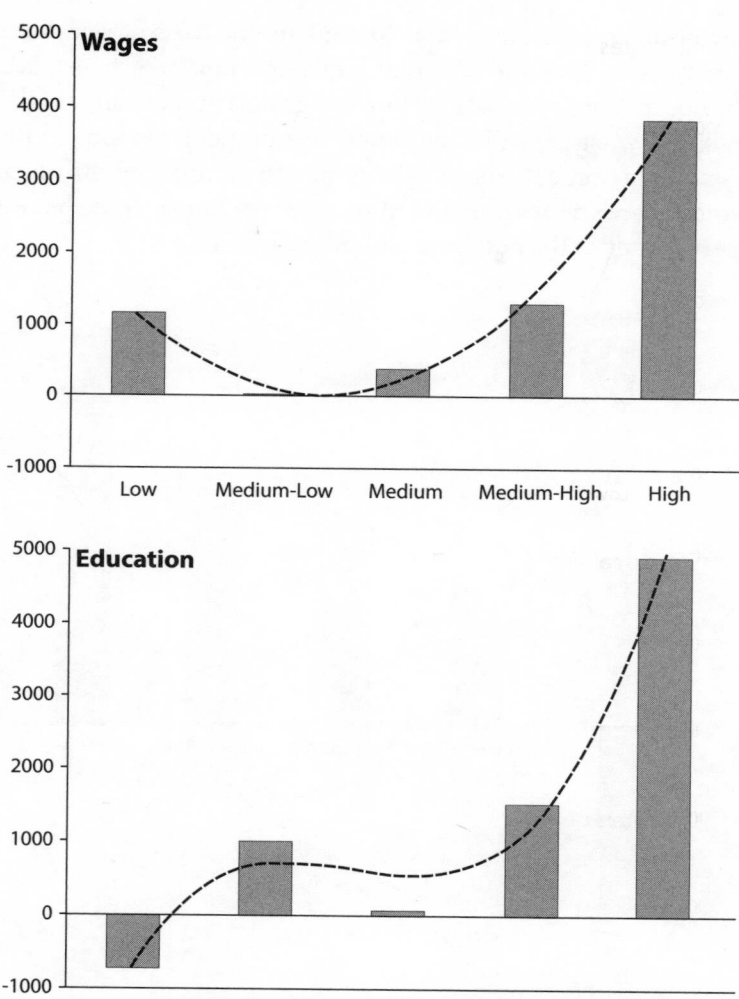

Figure 5.2b Net Job Creation or Destruction (in Thousands) in the (pre-Brexit) European Union, 2011–16, in Five Quintiles of Occupations Ranked by Education

Source and methodology: European Job Monitor, version of 18 December 2018 (consulted 21 January 2019).

Key: Between 2008 and 2010, employment fell by 380,000 in the lowest-waged occupations in Europe, and by 2.26 million in occupations where the workers were least educated on average.

and 2010, and then from 2011 to 2016, on the basis of workforce surveys by income and educational qualification. In each instance, the occupations are classified into five groups numerically similar in size – what are called quintiles. The first corresponds to the worst-paid occupations on average, and to occupations for which workers are the least qualified on average; conversely, the last corresponds to the best-paid and most qualified.

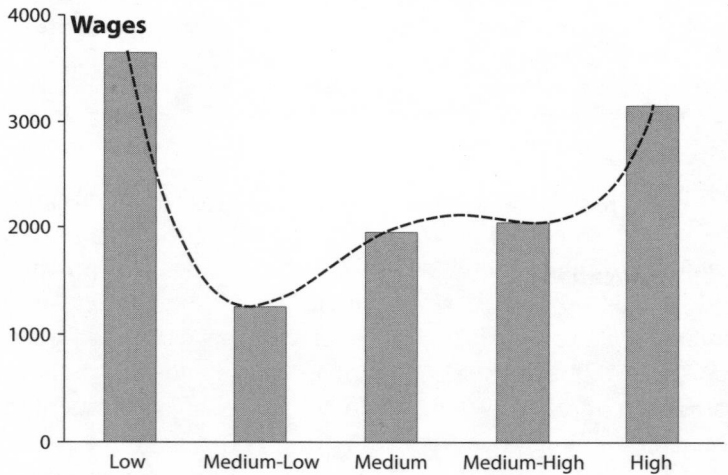

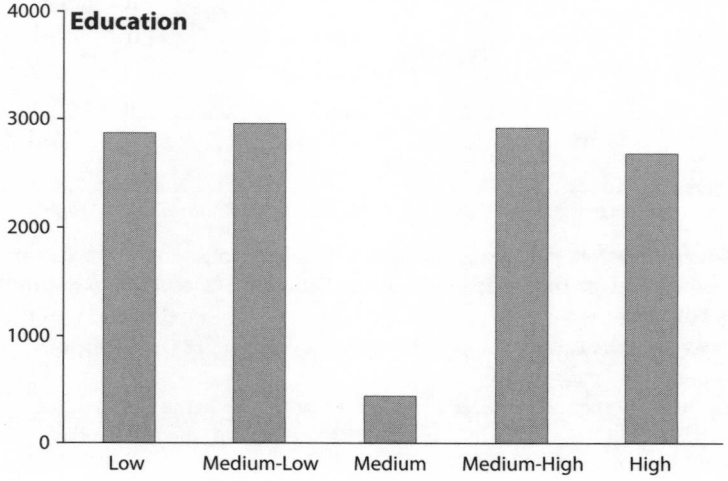

Figure 5.3 Net Job Creation (in Thousands) in the United States, 2012–17, in Five Quintiles of Occupations

Source: Author's calculations from data transmitted by the BLS, 11 October 2018; matching of employment projections 2012–22 and Occupational Employment Statistics for 2012 and 2017.

Field: Eight hundred occupations representing around 95 per cent of net job creation from 2012 to 2017.

Methodology: The occupations are classified into five quintiles in accordance, respectively, with level of average annual full-time wage in 2012 and level of education of those over the age of twenty-five in 2010–11. The occupations are weighted by their numbers in 2012.

Key: Between 2012 and 2017, employment increased by 3.7 million in the lowest-wage occupations in the United States, and by 2.9 million in occupations where workers were less educated on average.

In wage terms, the polarization of the European labour market was spectacular from 2008 to 2010. Employment collapsed for medium-low and low wages, and to a lesser extent for medium-high wages; low-wage employment held up and high-wage employment expanded. The period of emergence from the crisis – 2011–16 – saw an increase in employment in all quintiles, but once again more marked at the bottom, and especially the top, of the occupational wages hierarchy.

Analysis using the criterion of level of education yields a quite different trajectory. At the height of the crisis, as on emergence from it, we observe not polarization but a spectacular upgrading: the size of each occupational quintile increases with the workers' educational level. Employment in occupations of the first quintile – those involving a less educated workforce – declined by more than 2 million in the EU from 2008 to 2010, and continued to drop during 2011–16.

A comparable exercise can be conducted on the basis of the US data from the BLS (Figure 5.3). From 2012 to 2017, employment increased in the five occupational quintiles, regardless of whether a wage or qualification criterion is applied. But a wage polarization is apparent once again: a clear majority of the jobs created are in occupations at the bottom and top of the wages hierarchy. If we now take level of education as our criterion, we do not find a general rise, as in Europe, but nor is there any obvious polarization. Certainly, the relative share of the median group declines, reduced by the destruction of jobs such as bank clerk and executive assistant. But this time medium-low and medium-high jobs increase more rapidly than the extremes.

These seemingly contradictory observations are the consequence, in particular, of the development of jobs in what tend to be female service occupations, which are 'average' in terms of qualifications but whose wages have plainly stalled. In the US case, the most massive example is that of nursing auxiliaries, whose number went up by 0.8 million between 2012 and 2017 according to BLS statistics: they figure in the lowest income decile but the fourth decile in terms of education. From this perspective, wage polarization is not evidence of some natural dynamic contributing to the growth in primary inequalities. Instead, it is a symptom of the rents extracted by high pay and capital from part of the world of work, which would otherwise occupy the middle of the wages hierarchy.

Transcontinental Wage Stagnation

The intensification of work and the rise in educational levels contrast with the evolution of the wages of the 'less skilled'. In this respect, more striking than growing inequality is the stagnation, even decline, in their pay and/or their cost to employers.

The French and US experiences might seem opposed.[1] On the American side, the lowest hourly wages, especially for males,

---

1   It is also often argued that the division of income is distorted in the United States, whereas it has remained stable in France. The share accruing to capital in value-added in the United States has thus increased by something in the order of 5 points since the start of the century. This observation seems resistant to changes in methodology (see Michael D. Giandrea and Shawn A. Sprague, 'Estimating the US Labor Share', *Monthly Labor Review*, February 2017). We find such a fall in many OECD countries. In France, by contrast, depending on the hypotheses employed, the conclusions differ. In all cases, the tax-optimizing behaviour of multinationals blurs the profit and

were lower in the mid 2010s than at the start of the 1980s.[1] On average, the hourly wage of cooking and cleaning jobs was $2.20 in 1979 and, in real terms (deflated by the consumer price index) remained at $2.20 in 1989, 1999 and 2008. In France, the lowest hourly wages benefited from the dynamic of the minimum wage (SMIC), gaining around ten points. The purchasing power of hourly SMIC initially stagnated from the 1980s to the transition to the thirty-five-hour week. Then, it rose essentially at the start of the century thanks to the decisions of Chirac's right-wing governments. Since the election of Sarkozy in 2007 has stagnated once again, including during the mandate of the centre-left President Hollande.

Taking account of the increasing precarity in France (see Chapter 2) alters the diagnosis considerably.[2] A large part of the wage-earning class does not receive pay throughout the year. Thus, in the last decade net income from labour – wages plus unemployment benefits – have declined for workers at the bottom of the income distribution.

Similarly, in terms of hourly wage costs for employers, developments in France and the United States are similar. As a result of institutional differences and the availability of sources, it is instructive to compare the standard cost of an employee on SMIC (decreased by the Crédit d'Impôt Competitivité Emploi, or CICE) with that of US employees in private-sector service occupations (auxiliary nurses, gardeners, and so on) which contain the highest

---

value-added statistics. The share of profits is thus probably underestimated in France and Germany, and overestimated in countries with 'friendly' tax regimes, such as Ireland. The spatial placement of value-added by the digital giants for accounting purposes accentuates the measurement bias. On account of these limitations, which can create an uncertainty of several percentage points in calculations of the labour share, I shall not employ these data here.

1   See the State of Working America website, at stateofworkingamerica.org.

2   Philippe Askenazy and Bruno Palier, 'France: Rising Precariousness Supported by the Welfare State', in Brian Nolan, ed., *Inequality and Inclusive Growth in Rich Countries* (Oxford: Oxford University Press, 2018), Chapter 6.

percentages of low wages on both sides of the Atlantic.[1] Figure 5.4 displays the evolution in real terms of the hourly wage cost of the French SMIC and the average hourly total compensation of service occupations from 2005 to 2017. Two curves per country are presented, depending on whether the cost is deflated by a consumer price index or by the GDP deflator.[2] According to the two indices, the wage cost of the SMIC slightly increased in France, whereas that of service occupations in the United States stagnated until 2012. The cost of labour at the SMIC level then declined, whereas the wages of service occupations experienced a slight rise from 2015 to 2017 in the United States.

In fact, the rise in France's SMIC was offset for employers by exemptions from welfare contributions in the years 1990 and 2000.[3] Introduction of the CICE in 2013 and the Responsibility Pact (additional exemptions from contributions), combined with the absence of a boost to SMIC, then significantly reduced the wage bill for French employers. Lower employers' social contributions for wages at the level of the minimum wage are fairly common among countries with higher minimum wages (Belgium, the UK, and so on).

---

1   This category covers employees outside retail and administrative work: health workers including auxiliary nurses and stretcher bearers; funeral services workers; protection officers; firefighters; caretakers; security and catering workers; cooks and kitchen porters; cleaning and maintenance workers; room attendants; gardeners – and so on.

2   Numerous series of aggregate prices based on various notions and methods are produced by statistical institutes. They generally yield very similar results. However, in a period of macroeconomic shock, they can diverge significantly. The consumer price index registers the change in the price of final-consumption goods and services, and the GDP deflator makes it possible to proceed from a nominal GDP to a volume GDP, in particular for calculating economic growth. Which index to employ to account for a real labour cost relevant to employers is a matter of much discussion. In fact, depending on the firm's activity, one or another might be more pertinent.

3   See Philippe Askenazy, *The Blind Decades: Employment and Growth in France, 1974–2014*, transl. Susan Emanuel (Oakland, CA: University of California Press, 2015).

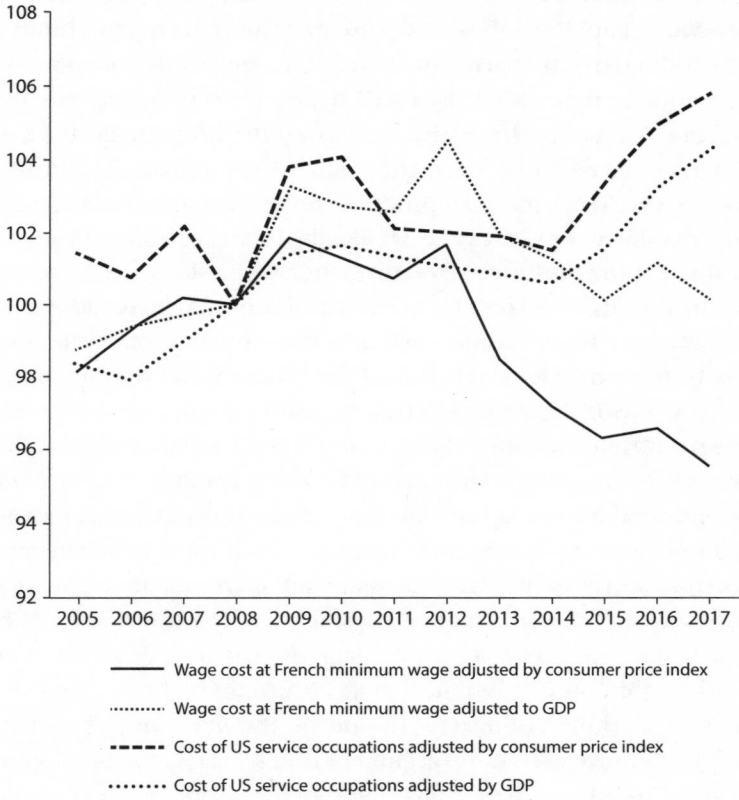

108
106
104
102
100
98
96
94
92

2005 2006 2007 2008 2009 2010 2011 2012 2013 2014 2015 2016 2017

——— Wage cost at French minimum wage adjusted by consumer price index

·········· Wage cost at French minimum wage adjusted to GDP

━ ━ ━ Cost of US service occupations adjusted by consumer price index

········ Cost of US service occupations adjusted by GDP

Figure 5.4 Wage Cost of Service Occupations in the United States and Deflated Estimates of the Wage Cost on SMIC (2005–17; base 100 = 2008)

Sources: Harmonized Eurostat Price Index for France; INSEE deflator of GDP – National accounts 2017; values of gross hourly SMIC, employers' contributions and CICE; Bureau of Labor Statistics total wage cost of private-sector service occupations and Consumer Price Index for urban consumers; Bureau of Economic Analysis GDP deflator (consulted 21 January 2019).

Key: Between 2008 and 2014, the cost for employers of an hour payed at SMIC dropped by 3 per cent in terms deflated by the harmonized consumer price index.

More Effort to Create Less Wealth?

The stagnation in labour costs is systematically justified by the low productivity of the 'less skilled' and, even more so, by the absence of productivity increases in their work, especially in services. The argument has been theorized by the US economist William Baumol for live performance: just as a symphony orchestra has done the same work since the end of the eighteenth century, today's cleaner or bin man produces no more than the cleaner or waste collector of yesteryear.[1] Unlike the financier, whose productivity has been multiplied by information technology, they are said to be outside the current industrial revolution. In the paradigm of productivity-based labour costs, it is therefore natural, even necessary, to arrange for stagnation of their wage bill for the employer.

This line of argument comes up against observation of work intensification and, more generally, of deterioration in the condition of these workers. How can more effort result in the creation of less wealth? Let us assume that productivity is indeed stagnant. This would mean that intensification does not translate into productivity increases; or that such increases are destroyed by occupational burn-out and de-skilling of the workforce. Such a socioeconomic system, which degrades the lives of millions of workers for nothing, is quite simply absurd. In that case, inequalities in working conditions should be the overriding political priority. Conversely, if the argument is false, it means (to adopt a Marxist term) that the surplus labour of the losers, or their casualization, creates rents appropriated by social groups of winners. In both cases, we reach the same conclusion: there is nothing natural about workers suffering a double penalty – increase in work pressures and stagnant wage compensation.

The veracity or otherwise of the argument implies different public policies and demands. So, is the productivity of 'less-skilled' workers, particularly in personal services, stagnating?

---

1   See William Baumol and William Bowen, *Performing Arts: The Economic Dilemma – A Study of Problems Common to Theater, Opera, Music, and Dance* (New York: Twentieth Century Fund, 1966).

The Poverty of Productivity Measurements

The answer to this question is obscured by considerable technical difficulties in measuring productivity. To fully address them would require an enormous collective effort, which nevertheless will not be undertaken in the absence of pressure from scholars and public authorities. The staff in the world's statistical services devoted to productivity are meagre. In the United States, the Bureau of Labor Statistics, which has to issue thousands of series, still only had a budget for seventy-five full-time positions in 2012. As in most OECD countries, fiscal austerity dictated a reduction in numbers. In 2016, the BLS had only fifty-eight full-time posts: statistical rigour was sacrificed to fiscal rigour.

Beyond these human resources considerations, the measurement of productivity poses major theoretical and practical problems. Here are a few illustrations of the point.

A first way of framing labour productivity, which unfortunately is unduly common in debates, is as nominal value-added per hour worked: the apparent productivity of labour.[1] If we use this indicator, we expose ourselves to a circular argument ('corresponding to low productivity is low labour cost'). The circularity is complete in the case of non-market services. In fact, nominal value-added in them is conventionally measured as the monetary sum of compensations, of taxes after subsidies, and the consumption of fixed capital (capital obsolescence): if wages and labour costs do not increase, neither does apparent productivity. The relationship between apparent productivity and wages is then purely numerical.

We find a significant circularity in market services for which prices are adjusted to remuneration, or even constitute that remuneration. Thus, the apparent value-added of a psychoanalyst is equal to the sum of payments by clients, reduced by the

---

1   The current international convention recommends a measurement of value-added at basic prices (invoice price minus the net total of taxes and subsidies on goods and services).

cost of overheads (electricity, housekeeping, and so on). If the psychoanalysts increase the price of consultations, and hence their remuneration, we will observe an apparent increase in their productivity.

The use of apparent productivity also results in strange situations that emerge from tax regimes. Let us take a cleaning lady working in Cannes for second-home owners. When she goes to the second home owned by an American resident, she receives the net sum (let us say) of €10 per hour, and her employer has to pay around €8 of social contributions in addition. Her hourly value-added, and hence her apparent productivity, is numerically €18. However, when she goes to the home of a working French resident, the latter will still pay €18, but will enjoy €9 of tax credit. The total employer cost of the hour worked is thus €9; and in national accounting (the current norm) the value-added is therefore €9. In short, the apparent productivity of the service delivery for the American is double what it is for the Frenchman, for exactly the same service and the same pay!

The fragility of the notion of apparent productivity explains the preference among economists for a different measure of productivity, expressed in volume terms. The idea is to ignore price effects and capture the volume of services or goods supplied. In the case of the cleaning lady in Cannes, her volume productivity will be the same with the French employer and the American; this is already significant progress! The statistical issue then becomes measuring this volume and tracking its development over time.

To harmonize calculations of the volumes produced, hundreds of pages of methodological recommendations have been issued by the OECD and Eurostat highlighting problems of measurement.[1] These still only tackle some of them. In Europe certain methods have been stipulated by European regulations,

---

1   Courageous readers can refer to OECD, *Measuring Productivity: OECD Productivity Manual – Measurement of Aggregate and Industry-Level Productivity Growth*, available at oecd.org.

particularly for education.[1] Ultimately, however, in each country statisticians have developed their own methods, dependent on the available sources, to try to calculate volume of production and volume of hours worked. Let us also note that, except in the case of individual activities, productivity is measured solely at the level of the establishment, business or branch of activity. In the case of a hospital, for example, output is the result of the intervention of a very large number of occupations: health professionals – from care assistants to practitioners – administrative support, maintenance, and so forth.

Let us return to the example of the cleaning lady in Cannes. INSEE, the French statistical service, possesses no source for directly calculating a volume of output. It therefore defines the volume produced by cleaning ladies as their wage bill divided by SMIC, the French minimum wage. If our lady in Cannes is paid above SMIC, and if her employers do not increase it, then a rise in SMIC will translate in the national accounts into a drop in her volume productivity! In such a schema, it is impossible

---

1   The volume produced in education is thus measured by the number of pupils weighted by a quality indicator for the whole of Europe, following a decision by the European Commission in December 2002. Quality is left to national statisticians to assess.

In France, quality is measured by success in exams: at a constant number of teachers, a rise in success in the *baccalauréat* translates into increased volume productivity. Yet the rate of success in the *baccalauréat* depends on ministerial directives on grading. In the last decade, the latter have tended to ensure a certain stability. In this case, the evolution of volume produced is essentially driven by the number of pupils. Consequently, when a government – for example, that of François Fillon during Nicolas Sarkozy's term – decides to abolish various elective courses, to abolish alternate positions, to reduce the network of help for pupils with special needs, and so on – at first sight a whole series of factors unconducive to quality, and even to the volume taught – the measured volume in productivity of teachers improves.

In the United Kingdom, success in exams being deemed too dependent on factors external to education (parents' social mobility, quality of housing, availability of crèches, access to municipal libraries, and so on), various measurements of the surplus-value of establishments are employed, but with a low weight: the key factor in the volume of education is the number of pupils.

to recognize technological progress. The cleaning appliances industry has made significant innovations: this is conveyed in the figures by an increase in the volume productivity of workers in this manufacturing sector. On the other hand, in the productivity of domestic services it will not be evident that the number of sheets cleaned in an hour by the cleaning lady is higher thanks to this technology.

In the inset, readers will find other examples of statistical conventions that conceal the sources of productivity. Having a bad thermometer is obviously frustrating. However, we can sketch an overview: current methods of calculation very largely ignore the development of the content and conditions of work. The effort contributed by part of the world of work is not conveyed in any statistic (Inset 1); worse, it may reduce their productivity or strengthen the performance measurement of other jobs (Inset 2). Jobs mostly done by women or minorities are particularly affected by such biases.

Inset 1: Condemned to Low Productivity

Domestic services are not the only activities conventionally condemned to being unproductive. Thus, in France the volume produced in retirement homes (classified among essentially non-market services) is the nominal value-added deflated by the wage evolution index: if the staff are more competent and more attentive – in short, if quality improves – the volume of production will be unchanged.

Even in some market services, the statistician does not always possess the requisite time and information. In the hospitality sector, for example, volume of production is assessed in most countries by the host's turnover deflated by a prices index for the consumption of hotel rooms or guestrooms. The advent of Booking.com and Airbnb has transformed the assessment of effective prices into a serious headache. Even prior to this

pitfall, however, accounting for quality effects was a very peril-
ous exercise. The statistician who observes a price increase will
ask the hotel if it has carried out improvements – for example,
making rooms larger or installing a swimming pool to obtain
an additional star. Often she will receive no answer. Worse, no
statistical body takes account of the quality effect prompted by
the battle of the beds. However, this is a major innovation of
this century in the upmarket hospitality trade. Competition has
set in around the quality of the bedding: beds are larger, mattresses often thicker and heavier, and there are more pillows. At
the same time, the staff must always be available and welcom-
ing to the clientele. Hence some occasionally impressive job
descriptions (see below). The result is a rise in the workload of
room attendants, which is invisible in the published productivity figures. Whether it is luxury hotels or the domestic cleaner,
the increase in volume produced, hence also economic growth,
is probably underestimated. At the same time, price rises in
services, which for the most part are consumed by the better-
off, are overestimated.

*Room Attendant Position at the Trump International
Hotel & Tower, Vancouver (accessed 10 January 2019)*

Location: Trump International Hotel & Tower, Vancouver
Department: Housekeeping
Job Code: RM 014
Employment Duration: Full-time

Description
Be Part of Our Exciting Team & Great Career Opportunities
We are looking for talented, caring individuals who would like
to be part of a progressive, customer centric, fun and passion-
ate company with great opportunities with one of the fastest
growing luxury hotel groups in the world.

Position Profile

The Room Attendant is responsible to maintain a high standard of cleanliness in guest rooms by ensuring they are properly supplied and free of maintenance problems in accordance with Hotel, Corporate and local standards. This position must adhere to all safety procedures, and follow all appropriate policies and procedures while constantly striving to improve all standards of operation. The Room Attendant must deliver prompt and courteous service to guests, ensuring all guest experiences are distinctively supreme.

Position Responsibilities

- Work in a safe manner and abide by Occupational Health & Safety legislation & the hotel's policies in regards to accident and incident reporting procedures.
- Report to the Housekeeping Shift Leader/Supervisor at the start and end of each shift.
- Abide by the policies and procedures as set out in the Associate Handbook and any other applicable Company policies.
- Wear the appropriate uniform as supplied by the hotel and appropriate footwear.
- Attend all scheduled shifts including shift work and weekend work in accordance with the schedules.
- Greet guest in a friendly and courteous manner during all interactions.
- Handle all guest interactions with the highest level of hospitality and professionalism.
- Work in any area assigned and complete any tasks as directed by the Housekeeping Shift Leader/supervisors, Director of Housekeeping and Management.
- Be pro-active in your approach to the job and work within the specific standards and procedures of The Trump International Hotel & Tower Vancouver.
- Attend all training sessions and meetings as required.
- Perform other duties/tasks and projects as assigned.

Position Requirements
- Strong communication skills both written and verbal.
- To be fluent in English both written and verbal. Proficiency in other languages would be an asset.
- Ability to follow all safety policies and procedures within work area and respond properly to any hotel emergency or safety situation.
- Ability to work well in a team environment.
- Ability to work well under pressure.
- Must adhere to the appearance and grooming policy.
- Flexibility and willingness to work overtime when necessary.
- Flexibility and willingness to work on a rotating schedule, including weekends and holidays.
- Ability to operate a handheld communication device.
- Ability to stand for extended periods of time.
- Ability to lift mattresses to properly make beds.
- Ability to carry a caddy of supplies weighing up to 10lbs.
- Ability to stand for extended periods of time and continuously perform the same essential job functions.

Education and Experience
Minimum 1 year working experience in a high level cleaning position. Room attendant experience is preferred.
High School diploma required.

From a scientific and statistical point of view, there is an enormous amount of work to be done to make a diagnosis, practically job by job, of the tasks performed and the output generated. It would facilitate a more relevant interpretation of work and the evolution of productivity, and hence of the springs of growth. In a different register, this interpretation would furnish a decisive lever for public action and workers' demands.

Inset 2: Retail Anomalies

Retail, which is essentially an industry of flows, approximates to an industrial concept of productivity. The measurement of volume of production is, at first blush, much easier than in the hospitality industry: sales volume is obtained by deflating the turnover by the price rises registered at sales points. Once again, however, this method ignores changes in work.

Thus, take the dealership of a major car manufacturer: quasi-systematically, the seller now offers finance through credit or by leasing the vehicle. Numerous manufacturers have created their own banks for customers: GM Financial, Toyota Financial Services, and so on. The car seller thus sells cars and credit at the same time. As of today, the latter task – the sale of a financial product – is not counted as contributing to the volume produced by the car dealership. On the contrary, these new credits are accounted in the output of the banking subsidiary, which in practice has no credit advisor for private individuals. Hence, some stratospheric results: for example, RCI, the bank of the Renault–Nissan group, and PSA bank post a credit output per employee that is ten times higher than that of traditional credit banking establishments (in France, Cofidis, Cetelem, and so on). Standard methods for calculating productivity thus involve the mutation of the occupation of car salesman into car dealership increasing productivity in … finance. Supermarkets will reveal another aspect of the meaning assumed by such figures.

Figure 5.5 presents the development of hourly productivity in volume on the basis of figures communicated by the Bureau of Labor Statistics for the years 1987–2017. How are we to interpret long-term increases of scarcely 13 per cent over twenty years when this segment has benefited from significant organizational and technological progress bound up with ICT?

The marked drop from 1987 to the mid 1990s can be explained by an extension in the opening hours and opening

Figure 5.5 The Strange Development of the Hourly Productivity of Labour in US Supermarkets, according to Bureau of Labor Statistics (1987–2017; base 100 = 2007)

Source: Series IPUHN44511_L000 (extracted 7 December 2018).

days of sales points. Numerous US states, from Texas to North Dakota, relaxed or even completely abolished the 'Blue Laws' that restricted shop opening on Sundays.[1] At the same time, daily opening hours were extended. This necessitated an increase in the volume of hours worked in supermarkets. However, the increase in turnover was not proportional. Since the measure of productivity in supermarkets is the flow of goods sold divided by the number of hours worked, measured productivity dropped. Quality is completely ignored: however, to be able to do one's shopping at any time represents an improvement

---

1   For an assessment of the economic effects of the Blue Laws, see, for example, Michael Burda and Philippe Weil, *Blue Laws* (2005) – pdf available at (ftp://ftp.cemfi.es/pdf/papers/wshop/BurdaBlue.pdf).

in the service offered by large food retailers. In the second half of the 1990s, the victory of Walmart and its 'big-box' stores, as well as the transformation of tasks at all levels described above, overcompensated for this opening-hours effect, initiating a re-ascending productivity curve.

Today's official statistical conventions play a doubly performative role. On the one hand, they neglect part of the productivity increases of the 'less skilled', creating a pretext for the characterization of low pay as natural, especially for women, migrants and minorities. On the other hand, they imprison the occupations in a hierarchy that is already staged by contemporary capitalism's winners. The 'unproductive' therefore face a triple non-recognition: of the degradation of their working conditions, of their increased productivity, and of the inadequacy of their pay. And, fundamentally, their critical role for the functioning of business and key services remains invisible.

6

Remobilizing Labour

The failure to recognize the men and women whose labour brings prosperity is not only damaging to democracy. It also condemns us to the deflationary spiral that lies at the heart of current crises. We are thus witnessing a new form of contradiction of capitalism which, in the name of competitiveness, is committing suicide. Major financial crises reveal this contradiction. Japan was the first country to fall into its own trap, in the closing decade of the twentieth century. During the 2008 crisis, US and UK leaders were determined to avoid the Japanese scenario by resorting to government debt and an injection of liquidity into the markets (zero interest rates, quantitative easing).[1] But wage stagnation in the United States and the persistent distortion of the allocation of value added in favour of profits, like the collapse of real wages in the UK, ended up cancelling the inflationary effects of these unconventional tools. A fall in sterling – a consequence of Brexit – and Trump's fiscal stimulus then fuelled slight price inflation, but without triggering strong wage growth. The Federal Reserve was even forced to cut its interest rate in 2019 despite low official

---

1   Ben Bernanke, previously an academic and author of analyses of the mistakes made by the Bank of Japan, was head of the US Federal Reserve when the financial and real-estate bubbles burst.

unemployment figures. For its part, the Eurozone remains bogged down in a pursuit of wage deflation. A schizophrenic European Central Bank (ECB) presses for 'structural reforms' in the labour market that undermine workers' bargaining power; these reforms ultimately prevent the ECB from achieving its objective of a stable inflation rate below, but close to, 2 per cent.

The Minimum Wage: A New Tool of the Conservatives

Conservative governments thus find themselves faced with an equation that is well-nigh impossible to solve: How to induce wage inflation without reversing the balance of power to the advantage of labour? For ideological reasons, they reject the state as employer increasing the wages of public employees. As a result, only one instrument is left to them: the minimum wage.

This might seem strange to French, Belgian, Swiss or North American readers, but the minimum wage is no longer a left-wing indicator. Some conservatives are keen on it. For them, the minimum wage has big advantages: it is controlled by the state, and can be frozen if necessary; it makes it possible to claim that active trade-union organizations can be dispensed with, and that workers' mobilizations are pointless, since the state guarantees the wages of the 'weakest', especially women.[1] Even large companies can use the minimum wage to that end. The $15 per hour applied by Amazon in the United States alone, represents an attempt to forestall criticism and demonstrations against the ultra-intensive working conditions that are a key source of its profits; it complements Amazon's active tactics against labour organizing. Basically, the promotion of the minimum wage by conservatives or giant companies can be interpreted as a fear of a potential reawakening of the working class.

---

1   But a minimum wage is far from sufficient to correct the scale of the occupational discrimination and segregation suffered by women. For France, see DARES, *Ségrégation professionnelle et écarts de salaires femmes-hommes*, *DARES analyses* 82 (November 2015).

Enthusiasm for the minimum wage also has its origins in the limits of monetary policy. The U-turn of the Cameron government, which included British Conservatives who were the inheritors of Margaret Thatcher, is worth lingering over. The Blairite government of Gordon Brown was in power when the global financial crisis exploded in 2008. In 2010, David Cameron's Conservatives succeeded it, initially in coalition with the centrist Liberal Democrats, and then on their own following the May 2015 general election. The UK was severely affected by the crisis as a result of its exposure to financial activities and the collapse of the housing market. It recovered to its pre-recession GDP only six years later – two years more than had been required to emerge from the depression of the 1930s. We can see why the 2008 crisis has been characterized in the UK as the 'Great Recession'.

Being outside the Eurozone, the UK retains control of its own monetary policy. Governments and the Bank of England were thus in a position to implement a coherent policy when confronted with the financial crisis. It consisted, on one hand, in organizing a rescue of the banking system and, on the other, in avoiding a surge in unemployment. The government deficit exploded, partially offset by an annual inflation rate of 4 per cent generated by monetary policy. The injection of liquidity made it possible to support the balance sheets of companies and adjust real wages. The objective was for inflation to 'eat up' wages, yielding a double dividend: first, the government would obtain a fall in the real wages bill for public servants without having to destroy jobs; second, the reduction in employers' labour costs would encourage them to retain their employees. In line with this same logic, the minimum wage would increase at a rate below that of inflation, while low-paid self-employment would receive a fiscal stimulus.

What government and the Bank of England had not anticipated was that wage adjustment would turn into a meltdown. The fall in bonuses of the top earners in the finance sector was expected – but the entire wages hierarchy collapsed by about 10/15 per cent in real terms between 2008 and 2012. The fall was marked for the low-paid, who found themselves on levels of real pay that returned them to where they had been in the first years of Thatcherism, three decades earlier.[1] Cameron and the Bank of England had ensnared themselves: they had not suspected the world of labour was so disarmed that it would accept impoverishment on this scale. Despite the economic recovery, the wages of the 90 per cent who form the 'bottom' of the hierarchy did not increase between 2012 and the time of writing, progressively plunging the economy into price stagnation. Even the drop in unemployment achieved nothing. Only house prices had begun to take off again, stimulated by zero interest rates and the resumption of bonuses in finance, giving rise to fears of the emergence of a new bubble.

Labour is so cheap that British firms are not incentivized to make productivity gains and invest. In the short term, this is conducive to employment; but in the medium term it will hamper growth.[2]

Re-elected in 2015, the Cameron government therefore had to contain the property boom, which was a vector of future macroeconomic instability; prevent the risk of a reaction by the world of labour that would be unwelcome to business and might favour the Labour Party; juggle the inflation that threatened stability and growth; and control the labour immigration that was translating into anti-European sentiment that would benefit the pro-Brexit populists of the UK Independence Party (UKIP).

As regards the risk of a new housing bubble, an end to zero interest rates was projected. To strangle any hint of industrial action at birth, Cameron passed anti-union legislation through parliament – which I shall return to below. Moreover, to counter the dangers bound up with deflation and immigration, he activated the minimum wage. An attempt was made to get firms to invest and increase prices by temporarily narrowing employers'

---

1   See Paul Gregg, Stephen Machin and Marina Fernández-Salgado, 'The Squeeze on Real Wages. And What It Might Take to End It', *National Institute of Economics Review* 228: 1 (2014).

2   See Alex Bryson and John Forth, 'The British Productivity Puzzle', in Philippe Askenazy, Lutz Bellmann, Alex Bryson and Eva Moreno Galbis, eds, *Productivity Puzzles across Europe* (Oxford: Oxford University Press, 2016).

margins through a wage rise controlled by the state. A controlled rise of the minimum wage was to yield miraculously rising wages and prices, stimulate investment, and deter the hiring of foreign workers (or at any rate east Europeans – UKIP's favourite targets).

Even in 2014, prior to his re-election, Cameron had significantly strengthened the arsenal of sanctions against employers who did not observe the minimum wage, with a policy of 'naming and shaming' – that is, publication of a list of offenders.[1] And it was not the department of labour but the tax authorities (HMRC) who were in charge of inspections: seventy new civil servants were recruited for the purpose. Once re-elected, Cameron decided to increase the penalties. Fines were raised to 200 times the value of the unpaid wages (with a ceiling of £20,000 per infringement); and company directors who did not obey the law could be banned from management for fifteen years. At the same time, on 1 October 2015, the minimum wage for those over the age of twenty-one, as well as that for eighteen-to-twenty-year-olds, was increased by 3 per cent, while the hourly minimum for apprentices went up by 21 per cent. At the start of 2016, a British apprentice below the age of eighteen received a minimum in his first year close to that of a French apprentice after three years.

More 'revolutionary' still, from April 2016, the minimum wage gave way to a 'living wage' (theoretically a wage sufficient to lead a decent life) for those over twenty-five.[2] At a stroke, the gross

---

1   For example, in 2015 a list of seventy firms was published: 'Government Names and Shames Largest Ever Number of National Minimum Wage Offenders', Department for Business, Innovation and Skills, 24 February 2015, at gov.uk.

2   The issue of the living wage is not new in British debates. Thus, we might cite the famous blistering intervention in 1909 of a young member of parliament, a certain Winston Churchill: 'It is a serious national evil that any class of His Majesty's subjects should receive less than a living wage in return for their utmost exertions. It was formerly supposed that the working of the laws of supply and demand would naturally regulate or eliminate that evil. The first clear division which we make on the question to-day is between healthy and unhealthy conditions of bargaining. That is the first broad division which we make in the general statement that the laws of supply and demand will

minimum wage for the majority of wage-earners rose from £6.70 an hour to £7.20.

The living wage was not a factor in the way the British voted during the EU referendum, but did it make it possible to restart the engine of wages in the UK? It was reasonable to be pessimistic in view of the Japanese experience. The minimum wage there is fixed within prefectures, but the central government decides on increases. Faced with persistent deflation, Japanese conservatives were won over to the 'benefits' of the minimum wage. In March 2007, the first government of Shinzo Abe organized a significant increase in minimum wages in all prefectures for 2008 – 3.7 per cent in the Tokyo prefecture, for example. On its return to power in 2012, the government did not deviate from this strategy. Between 2007 and 2015, the nominal hourly minimum wage rose by 12 per cent in the Tottori prefecture (in the south-west of the island of Honshu) and by 23 per cent in that of Tokyo, while cumulative inflation in these years was a mere 3 per cent. The increases have continued since, but inflation has still not taken off in Japan. Basically, the minimum wage is too weak as a macroeconomic tool, because it only benefits those at the bottom of the wages hierarchy.

---

ultimately produce a fair price. Where in the great staple trades in the country you have a powerful organisation on both sides, where you have responsible leaders able to bind their constituents to their decision, where that organisation is conjoint with an automatic scale of wages or arrangement for avoiding a deadlock by means of arbitration, there you have a healthy bargaining which increases the competitive power of the industry, enforces a progressive standard of life and the productive scale, and continually weaves capital and labour more closely together. But where you have what we call sweated trades, you have no organisation, no parity of bargaining, the good employer is undercut by the bad, and the bad employer is undercut by the worst; the worker, whose whole livelihood depends upon the industry, is undersold by the worker who only takes the trade up as a second string, his feebleness and ignorance generally renders the worker an easy prey to the tyranny of the masters and middle-men, only a step higher up the ladder than the worker, and held in the same relentless grip of forces – where those conditions prevail you have not a condition of progress, but a condition of progressive degeneration.' Trade Boards Bill, HC Deb, 28 April 1909, col. 388.

This is what has also been seen in the UK since the introduction of the living wage; but the latter has nevertheless had a significant impact at the bottom of the wages hierarchy. Despite the fall of Cameron with the victory of Brexit, the Conservatives have accelerated the rise in the living wage, so that it will reach 60 per cent of the median wage by 2020. The British Low Pay Commission provides numerous statistics on the impact of this sharp rise on the distribution of wages and jobs. Not only the lowest earners have enjoyed wage increases. There was a ripple effect: the wages of the first quartiles in the salary distribution have increased at a nominal rate twice that of wages in the other quartiles. Even those under twenty-five benefited from this dynamic, because firms had a tendency to award them increases in line with their elders. In short, inequalities in hourly wages have significantly narrowed in the UK.

Similar dynamics can be observed in Germany. The conservative Angela Merkel readily accepted the 'demand' by the German Social Democratic Party for a minimum wage to be introduced progressively in Germany, starting in 2015. Since then, the coalition has revalued this minimum wage every two years uncontroversially, in line with the proposals of a mixed committee of employers and trade unions.

The consequences of these policies for the total volume of employment appear statistically marginal in the UK, Japan and Germany.[1] Likewise, the French CICE, which on the contrary represents a drop of some 6 per cent in labour costs (for jobs paid up to 250 per cent of the SMIC), has probably had only a marginal positive effect on employment, at best.[2]

In a neoclassical model of the labour market, these observations are compatible with a monopsony situation – that is, one

---

1   See, for example, O. Bruttel, A. Baumann and M. Dütsch, 'The New German Statutory Minimum Wage in Comparative Perspective: Employment Effects and Other Adjustment Channels', *European Journal of Industrial Relations* 24: 2 (2018).

2   Monitoring committee – of which the author was a member – on the Crédit d'Impôt pour la Competitivité et l'Emploi, *Rapport 2018* (Paris: France Stratégie, 2018).

in which the direct or indirect employer has a monopoly on the supply of jobs to workers in a given sector. The employer can then extract a rent by paying wages beneath their competitive level.[1]

From the Myth of the End of the Wage-Earning Class to Its New Criticality

While conservatives may be unable to resolve the ideological contradictions of their economic policy, European social democracy is undeniably in crisis. Overtaken on its left flank, paralysed by the rise of varieties of populism, it is struggling to re-found itself intellectually while invoking pragmatism. Unfortunately, this endeavour is based on often mistaken views of the economy and society, to the point where it results in the conviction that only a radicalized Blairite way holds out a future for social democracy. In France, this conviction was particularly deep-rooted in the circles around the former socialist governments.[2] The success of Jeremy Corbyn in the Labour Party leadership election in September 2015 is even interpreted on both sides of the Rhine not as the result of a radical rejection of Blairism, but as the delayed consequence of the Iraq operation in 2003. Furthermore, it is argued in conferences on the future of social democracy, most Labour members of parliament remain attached to a Blairite economic and social vision.

Blairism is often caricatured by the 'left of the left' as pure economic liberalism. In fact, it involved a new coalition of social groups around equality of opportunity. The goal of equality (of income, wealth, working conditions) is abandoned, deemed unattainable or unwanted by society. Opposing the liberal dynamic is therefore pointless. On paper, economic liberalism can even permanently shake up vested interests, offering opportunities for all. If the snapshot of inequalities at a particular time t is

---

1   I shall return to concrete situations of monopsony in the following sections.

2   The book by Philippe Aghion, Gilbert Cette and Élie Cohen, *Changer de modèle* (Paris: Odile Jacob, 2014), is an example of 'radical Blairism'.

unchanged, equality of opportunity is bound to enable upward social mobility for some at the price of social descent for others. From this perspective, public effort must focus on individuals, not the collective. In particular, young people must enjoy support- ive conditions. Under Blair, Labour thus beefed up transfers to families with children. Hundreds of thousands of employees were recruited in education and health, with the blessing of employers, who needed trained, healthy young people.

However, this progressivism soon comes up against primary inequalities. In allowing these to drift, it becomes divorced from equality of opportunity. The primary determinant of the oppor- tunities of a new-born is the status of its parents as defined by income, wealth, housing, networks, and so forth. The failure to provide equality of opportunity is patent in the United Kingdom, where only one-quarter of poor workers succeed in escaping poverty after ten years of work. In addition, the latest sociolog- ical work detects no progress in terms of social mobility. Worse, the upwards mobility of the middle classes would seem to have declined, while their downward mobility has increased.[1] The dom- ination of Oxbridge within the economic, political and intellectual elites is increasingly overwhelming. Even in elite sport, the chil- dren of the best-off assert themselves.[2]

Let us return to France – the only major European power that, at the time of Donald Trump's election, had had a self- declared social-democratic government in post for several years. A 'neo-Blairite' analysis had prevailed within it. The emblematic

---

1   Erzébet Bukodi, John H. Goldthorpe, Lorraine Waller and Jouna Kuha, 'The Mobility Problem in Britain: New Findings from the Analysis of Birth Cohort Data', *British Journal of Sociology* 66: 1 (2015), pp. 93–117.

2   In 2012, the UK played host to the London Olympic Games, which had been secured by Tony Blair (who had arrived in 10 Downing Street in 1997); the athletes of the Blair generation lined up. The UK came third in the medal table – a major success. But of the sixty-five medal-winners, twenty-four were products of fee-paying private schools, which are attended by only 7 per cent of young Britons. Hailing from such a school made an athlete almost six times as likely to win a medal than those from state schools – the same inequality of opportunity as for becoming a member of parliament.

economics minister, Emmanuel Macron, denounced 'egalitarianism' and promoted equality of opportunity. The law he defended in 2015 was entitled 'For growth, activity and equality of opportunity'. We can identify a stress on education in French policy, even if the effort mobilized was considerably less than that across the Channel under Blair.

But the project aspires to be more radical. It is rooted in a dual analysis: not only are inequalities natural; the wage-earning class is inexorably disappearing. In Chapter 2, I stressed its slow fragmentation in many countries, associated with the advance of short-term contracts and temping. It is now supposedly destined to die. 'Uberized', the world of work will become a sum total of individual entrepreneurs, moving from the legal status of employee (private or public) to self-employed status, in line with opportunities. In light of this, we must register a second defeat: there is no possibility of any collective workers' movement.

The only solution is equality of opportunity and, beyond Blairism, the creation of new rights for the individual to organize her occupational transitions. Such is the logic of the 'personal activity account' in France: 'For each person to possess as of 1 January 2017 an account ... which, from their entry into the labour market and throughout their working life, independently of their status, assembles the personal social rights conducive to securing their professional career' (training, unemployment benefit, holidays). The principle is as follows: in a world where workers are summoned to become entrepreneurs, they must enjoy rights that enable them to be entrepreneurs on their own behalf.

Emmanuel Macron's election to the French presidency in 2017 ensured the survival of this project. Even if the conditions will be restrictive, self-employed people who have gone into liquidation, and wage-earners who have resigned or are being retrained, will be able to access the unemployment benefit hitherto reserved to employees who have been dismissed. Conversely, as already signalled, the labour law of autumn 2017 introduced into France quasi-employment-at-will of the US variety. It drastically limits worker protections against dismissal, above all making it harder to win compensation in the case of unfair dismissal and asserting that employees made redundant shall not be rehired. What unfairly dismissed employee with less than a year's tenure is going to go to court to obtain compensation amounting to, at most, a month's salary?[1]

While they aim to respond to the individualization of career paths, such individual rights risk undermining any collective approach on the part of labour. That is why it is necessary to be certain that the working class is doomed to disappear before fixing its components. For some countries, a simple continuation of recent trends gives credence to this idea. We have seen it with zero-hour contracts in the UK, or the millions of contracts shorter than a week in France. Wherever simplified regimes of entrepreneurship exist (*zelfstandigen zonder personeel* in the Netherlands, and so on), self-employed jobs have expanded significantly since the start of the crisis.

Nevertheless, the trend is far from general. For the whole EU, whether with fifteen members or twenty-eight, the share of self-employed work has crumbled in the last decade, according to the European Workforce survey. It has declined markedly in Germany and Italy. If we confine ourselves to self-employed workers without any employees, we observe a moderate increase in the fifteen-member EU, rising from 9.5 per cent of those in active employment just before the Great Recession to 9.7 per cent in the second quarter of 2018, according to Eurostat data. But if we remove France, the UK and the Netherlands, their share has continued to fall in the rest of the European Union. These observations suggest that it is the policies implemented in certain countries that usher in a new phase in the de-structuring of the world of labour, rather than it being a natural phenomenon they assist.

---

1   In late 2018 and early 2019, courts of the first instance refused to apply these scales, which were held in particular to contravene convention 158 of the ILO on dismissal (the convention referred to in Chapter 2). Eventually, the French high civil court determined in mid 2019 that these scales were consistent with the international treaties ratified by France. The next step will be decisions of international courts.

To gain a clearer view of things, it is useful to cross the Atlantic. After all, Uber and Airbnb come from the United States, and the US labour market is an archetype of flexibility (with the least rigidity according to OECD indicators) and facility of entrepreneurship. The Bureau of Labor Statistics furnishes the shares in total employment of the self-employed (whether with company status or not), as well as the proportion of persons with several jobs (which partially covers the first category).[1] Since 2005, if there is a trend, it is rather towards the decline of self-employed work or an accumulation of jobs, and not (as is sometimes fantasized in Europe) an inexorable decline in waged main employment.[2] Likewise, according to the national accounts, the mixed income of the totality of the self-employed – in their main or secondary job – does not evince a clear pattern, diminishing from a little over 10 per cent of total gross value-added in 2005 to 9.2 per cent in 2010, before recovering to 10 per cent since 2012 (beneath its 2001 peak).[3]

Other BLS data makes it possible to get a more precise handle on 'alternative work arrangements' (Table 6.1). In addition to individual entrepreneurs, they pertain to three categories: workers on demand, workers made available by a contracting firm, and temporary jobs. Until 2005, the BLS collected data through a vast survey of several thousand workers, the Current Population Survey (CPS). The halting of this data collection led two of the most prestigious US labour economists, Lawrence Katz and Alan Krueger, to carry out their own survey of around 2,200 workers in

---

1   Self-employed workers are those identified by the question: 'Last week, were you employed by government, by a private company, a nonprofit organization, or were you self-employed?'

2   In detail, self-employed work in the form of a company is rather stable, whereas the size of unincorporated self-employment is in decline.

3   Among the other G7 countries, the size of mixed income in 2017 was similar to that of 2005 in Canada and the UK, and in decline in Japan (to less than 4 per cent), the United States, Germany, and Italy, where it remains the largest, at 15 per cent of value-added. OECD national accounts, accessed 9 January 2019.

Table 6.1 Alternative Work Arrangements in the USA (2005–17, as a Percentage)

Survey	1995 CPS	2005 CPS	2015 RAND	2017 CPS
Independent contractors	6.7	7.4	8.4 to 9.6	6.9
On-call workers	1.7	1.8	2.6 to 2.8	1.7
Temporary help agency workers	1.0	0.9	1.6	0.9
Workers provided by contract firms	0.5	0.6	3.1 to 3.3	0.6
Total	9.9	10.6	15.8 to 17.2	10.1

Sources: Lawrence F. Katz and Alan B. Krueger, 'The Rise and Nature of Alternative Work Arrangements in the United States, 1995–2015', *Industrial and Labor Relations Review* 72: 2 (2019); Bureau of Labor Statistics, Current Population Survey (consulted 9 January 2019).

2015, financed by the RAND Corporation. From it they obtained a remarkable result: the share of workers in an alternative work arrangement had grown spectacularly in 2015 (RAND column in Table 6.1). This finding immediately sparked considerable debate. It was said to constitute proof of a mutation in employment in the United States. The scale of the mutation resulted in examination of the relevance of creating new statuses between pure self-employed work and waged work, such as, for example, that of 'para-subordinate' in Italy.[1]

The need to track this phenomenon compelled the BLS to resume its collection of information from a CPS sample that was much more representative than the RAND-Princeton Contingent Survey. And (surprise, surprise!) the 2017 survey, which involved 60,000 US households, contradicted the results of Katz and Krueger: there was no apparent growth spurt in alternative work arrangements (CPS columns in Table 6.1).

---

1   Seth D. Harris and Alan B. Krueger, *A Proposal for Modernizing Labor Laws for Twenty-First-Century Work: The 'Independent Worker'*, Hamilton Project Discussion Paper 2015-10 (2015).

Table 6.2 United States: Tenure of Employees with Current Employer from January 1996 to January 2018 (in years); and Share of Private Sector Employees in Firms with More than 100 Employees, from First Quarter 1996 to First Quarter 2018 (as a Percentage)

	Tenure less than a year	*Tenure 10 years or more*	*10 years or more (workers aged 25 or more)*	*Salaried in firm with 100 or more employees*
1996	26.0	25.8	30.5	60.6
1998	27.8	25.8	30.7	61.8
2000	26.8	26.6	31.7	62.4
2002	24.5	26.2	31.0	62.1
2004	23.0	26.0	30.6	61.7
2006	24.4	25.6	30.0	62.1
2008	22.9	27.1	31.5	62.7
2010	19.0	28.8	33.1	62.8
2012	21.1	29.2	33.7	63.3
2014	21.3	29.1	33.3	63.7
2016	22.6	28.9	33.2	64.1
2018	22.3	28.8	33.2	64.6

Sources: Bureau of Labor Statistics, Tenure of American Workers, Spotlight on Statistics (September 2013), Employee Tenure 2018, 2016, 2014 and 2012, Quarterly Data Series on Business Employment Dynamics (accessed 7 December 2018).

Within the ranks of the wage-earning class itself, it is also hard to see an implosion in the direction of very short-term jobs. If, for a given age group, median tenure with the same employer declined in the 1980s and 1990s, the trend was reversed between the start of the century and 2014, according to BLS data. More precisely, the data show an increase for women and a stabilization for men. For example, the median tenure of men aged between thirty-five and forty-four fell from 7.3 years in January 1983 to 5.1 in January 2002, settling at 5.4 years in January 2014 before dipping to 5 in 2018. In short, the percentage of US employees with less than a year's tenure with their current employer has been in decline since the start of the century, while the share of those with at least ten years is growing.

Furthermore, only 4.8 per cent of US waged employment in the private sector in 2018 (apart from direct employment by private individuals and small agricultural units) was in firms with fewer than five employees. Conversely, employment in firms with more than 100 employees has continued to increase, exceeding 64 per cent of total private employment in 2018. The rise is even clearer in large firms of more than 1,000 employees, which in 2018 accounted for more than 40 per cent of private waged employment, as against 36 per cent in 1996.[1] Once again, these data do not include employees of the small subcontractors of these large firms, or those of franchises. Much more so than the disappearance of the wage-earning class, the key economic, social and legal issue is the rupture in the bond of subordination. In other words: 'Who's the boss?'

Overall, the proportions are similar in France – part of a long-term trend of increasing domination by large firms. In 2016, according to INSEE, the 292 largest French businesses (more than 5,000 employees) employed nearly 30 per cent of the business sector (not counting jobs in their franchises). French and foreign multinationals employ nearly half of private-sector employees. These developments are consistent, on one hand, with the propertarianism in intangible assets that confers a premium on the most powerful firms and, on the other, with the concentration of productive activities. The wage-earning class in large organizations – directly employed, subsidiary, franchisee or sub-contractor – is therefore not becoming extinct. Quite the reverse. Theoretically, this leaves open the possibility of collective mobilization.

But can wage growth be stimulated in order to escape deflation and favour justice, in terms of the recognition of labour and its conditions? How can labour be remobilized in the context of democracy and the market economy? Should traditional trade unionism be reactivated, or do new forms of mobilization need to be invented?

---

1   Economists refer to the granularity (as opposed to atomization) of the economy when it is based on a few big firms.

An extensive academic literature has studied a large variety of paths towards union renewal.[1] By contrast, I explore here the criticality as a generic catalyst for the revitalization and success of labour movements.

Working-Class Trade Unionism and the Conservative Obsession

I have already highlighted the dynamic of de-unionization and, more generally, erosion of the power of labour unions. However, trade-union bastions survive that employ methods similar to those of corporations. But unlike corporations, which are sometimes represented in the legal form of a syndicate, the activity of working-class trade unions claims to benefit several occupations, not a particular body; and they are affiliated to inter-occupational movements.[2] Whereas the corporations originating in regulated professions form electoral battalions for conservative parties (doctors, bailiffs), and are feared by some social-democratic parties, what remains of the labour movement is naturally combated by conservatives and liberals.

These are bastions where unions are in a position to demonstrate their criticality by striking and the employer may dispose of monopolistic rents.[3] Their criticality is thus equal to the probability of strikes multiplied by losses; the losses are incurred directly by the employer (and, in the case of public services, by the whole economy). Thus, the metro networks of the great metropolises evince exceptional levels of criticality on account of the scale of potential losses.

---

1   For a review, see G. Murray, 'Union Renewal: What Can We Learn from Three Decades of Research?', *Transfer: European Review of Labour and Research* 23: 1 (2017): 9–29.

2   In France, for example, the Syndicat National des Pilotes de Ligne only defends pilots in organizations such as Air France, where they account for less than 10 per cent of the staff.

3   As I have already emphasized, various works note statistically that the premium for a trade-union presence increases with the rents of firms.

Let us take three global cities: New York, London and Paris. In all three cases, most metro lines are controlled by a public or quasi-public operator. However, on account of their considerable geographical expanse, New York and London are much more sensitive to the functioning of their network than Paris, where distances are considerably shorter.[1] Rail transport congestion is also more acute in the first two cities. Accordingly, even partial strike action in London or New York generates potential losses far in excess of those suffered by Paris.

In addition, the Metropolitan Transport Authority in the United States confronts a single trade union comprising more than half of the staff: local 100 of the Transport Workers' Union of America (TWU). The majority of operatives on London Underground, including drivers, are likewise affiliated to a trade union to defend their demands when dealing with Transport for London. The union scene there is more fragmented, with four unions (Unite, ASLEF, TSSA and RMT). However, it has been dominated for more than a decade by the National Union of Rail, Maritime and Transport Workers (RMT). In 2002, the RMT elected a leader, Bob Crow, who defined himself as a socialist and was well-known for the bust of Lenin displayed in his office.[2] He implemented a trade-union strategy based on increased strike calls, often translated into action, particularly on the London underground. In fact, he significantly enhanced the level of his union's criticality while its membership grew.

The Régie Autonome des Transports Parisiens (RATP) benefits from a trade-union scene that is much more fragmented, with no less than eight organizations present in the latest workplace elections. None of them obtains more than one-third of the votes, or has a charismatic leader.

In short, in New York agents have a high level of criticality – hence their considerable bargaining power. It is also very

---

1   The population densities of inner London and New York City are close to 11,000 inhabitants per square kilometre, as against more than 20,000 for Paris.

2   Bob Crow died in 2014 and was replaced by his deputy.

Table 6.3 Gross Annual Wages in 2015 (Bonuses Included) of Full-Time Metro Drivers on the New York, London and Paris Networks (National Currency)

	Starting trained driver	*Maximum*
New York	~ $65,000	~ $100,000 to $200,000
London	~ £48,000	~ £60,000
Paris	~ €30,000	~ €50,000

Sources: Websites of ASLEF, TfL, and TWU and seethroughny.net (site of conservative think tank Empire Center, which publishes the individual salaries of New York public servants in accordance with the laws on transparency in public administrative information); author's estimates from RATP's pay scales (available on the site of the UNSA RATP) and informal individual interviews with RATP agents; data extracted 23 August 2015.

significant in London, where agreements in the wake of conflicts and strike threats have multiplied since the start of the century. By contrast, the Paris network is characterized by lower potential losses and a weak trade-union scene.

How do these differences play out when it comes to pay? Comparison between the conditions of agents on the three networks is difficult. In addition to wages proper, they enjoy benefits in terms, for example, of additional healthcare cover and social services. However, examination of drivers' wages exclusively is informative. Table 6.3 is confined to the gross pay of full-time metro drivers in the three companies in 2015. The agents perform relatively similar tasks and experience cumulative pressures on the three networks: isolation, confinement, artificial lighting, an atmosphere saturated with fine particles, unsocial working hours, responsibility, and 'customer contingencies' (physical attacks, suicides, and so on).

At the end of his or her career, a Paris metro driver has not attained the annual wage of a debutant in London or New York. It should be made clear that short working hours in Paris are insufficient to generate such massive differences. Thus, with a working week of thirty-seven and a half hours and forty-three days of paid holidays, the London driver works around 10 per cent more than his Parisian counterpart. The TWU and the four London

Underground trade unions are able to obtain better pay, which is very similar in terms of parity purchasing power.

Ultimately, a London Underground driver earns roughly 50 per cent more than an English pharmacist, and a New York Subway driver around one-third less than a salaried pharmacist in the metropole of New Jersey.[1] A Parisian Metro driver, meanwhile, earns one-third the amount of a French pharmacist.

In short, classical trade unionism pays, but it struggles to conquer significant new bastions because it is too bound up with the characteristics of the workplaces where it is practised.[2] Furthermore, conservative forces know full well how to instrumentalize the most acute conflicts so as to turn public opinion against trade unions. In this respect, recurrent strikes on the London Underground were a godsend for the Cameron government in the UK. With the return of pseudo–full employment, British trade unions, like industrial relations specialists, pondered ways of reconquering the world of work. Hence the support given by the major unions to Jeremy Corbyn, the left-wing Labour MP, for the party's leadership. For the post-Thatcher Tories, preventing any resurgence of trade unionism was a priority. Following his re-election, Cameron therefore initiated the process of new anti-union legislation. Unwisely, the Conservatives went so far as to require union leaders to wear armbands on picket lines, on penalty of heavy fines: armbands for trade unionists had been introduced by Hitler in the first concentration camp in Dachau in 1933, British unions protested. Ultimately, the law enacted in spring 2016 stipulated that a projected strike has to be adopted by a ballot in the relevant enterprise, with at least 50 per cent of

---

1   According to the data of the Bureau of Labor Statistics, the average annual salary of a pharmacist in 2014 in the metropolitan region of New York-White Plains-Wayne was $117,000.

2   Beyond the case presented, Anglo-American statistical work in quantitative economics and sociology alike converges in disclosing a wage premium. See, for example, Bruce Western and Jake Rosenfeld, 'Unions, Norms, and the Rise in US Wage Inequality', *American Sociological Review* 76 – and, below, the cases of nurses, room attendants or coach drivers.

trade unionists voting; in public services (transport, health, and so on), a minimum of 40 per cent of the electorate has to vote for the strike. In addition, firms can hire temporary staff to break the strike. Despite this rigid standard, strikes, particularly on the British rail network, have since been numerous. Their staggered character, with a non-continuous schedule on different days of the week, maximizes service disruption and reduces the ability of companies to circumvent them.

In France, it was the damage caused by individuals on the margins of trade-union demonstrations that served as a pretext for a Senate bill proposed in 2018 by the most conservative fringe of the Republicans. Adopted by the government of Emmanuel Macron, which cited the confrontations between the Yellow Vests and Interior Ministry forces, the bill was also passed by the National Assembly in February 2019. The police will be able to frisk people more easily and resort to 'preventive' detention in advance of any demonstration, including by trade unions. The most liberticidal provision of the law was censured by the Conseil Constitutionnel (supreme constitutional court): the *préfet* (local representative of the state) would have been empowered to ban from demonstrating any person he deemed to be 'a particularly serious threat to public order'.

While these authoritarian reactions can muzzle traditional trade unionism, it is more difficult for them to counter all forms of mobilization. Trade unionism is in fact putting forth new buds that, while they remain limited, are potentially inspirational.

A New Trade Unionism of Opinion

Let us return to our comparison of nurses with pharmacists – this time in the United States. Figure 6.1 compares the hourly wage of registered nurses (excluding anaesthetist nurses and nurse managers) with the hourly wage of pharmacists in various US states. This comparison makes it possible to exclude local effects, such as cost of living and health needs.

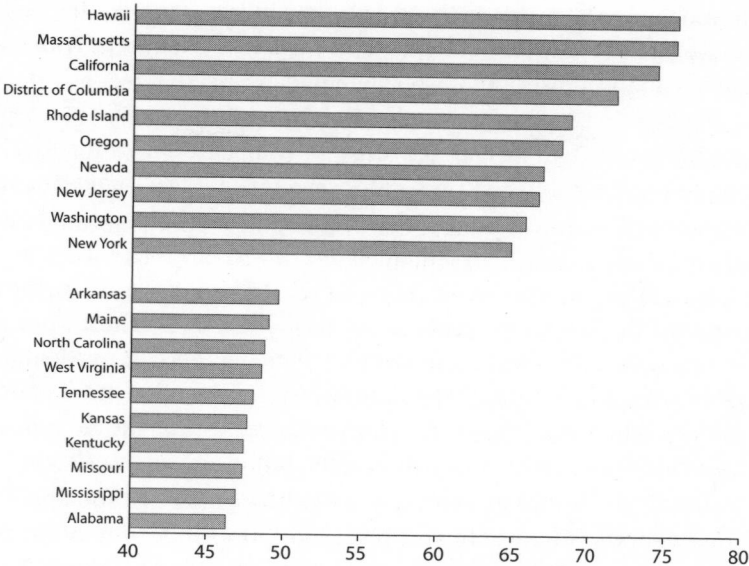

Figure 6.1 Hourly Wages of Nurses Compared with the Wages of Pharmacists in the United States (as a Percentage, May 2014). Ten States with the Highest and Ten States with the Lowest Relative Wages

Source: Author's calculations from occupational employment statistics of the Bureau of Labor Statistics (accessed 5 October 2015).

The differences are considerable. In some states, essentially those of the southern and central United States, the hourly wage of nurses is half that of pharmacists, whereas it rises to three-quarters in Hawaii, California and Massachusetts. How do we explain that the wage of nurses in Maine is one-third lower than in Massachusetts, both of them north-western states separated by the New Hampshire corridor by a mere fifty kilometres? Once more, the argument that wages reflect a 'natural' difference linked to productivity seems hard to sustain.

In May 2014, there were 2.7 million employed US nurses. Their rate of unionization was rather high by US standards, at close to 20 per cent. The principal union derived from the merger in 2009 of several organizations under the banner of National Nurses United (NNU). It claims almost 190,000 members, and its affiliated organizations have experienced a marked increase in membership in the last two decades (in excess of the demographic growth of the occupation prompted by growing health needs).

US health institutions, whether public or private (profit-making or non-profit-making), are covered by the National Labor Relations Board, established under Roosevelt's New Deal. The Board is responsible, in particular, for organizing workplace elections when a trade union is present and can compel employers to negotiate with the unions. A decision of the Supreme Court in 1991 required the Board to create occupational colleges. Thus, nurses form a separate college from doctors, which allows, in particular, for the election of nurses' representatives despite opposition from doctors when this measure was introduced. Since the Supreme Court decision, elections have proliferated in the health sector.

But the NNU has developed a strategy that goes beyond the traditional balance of power. Whereas public-transport unions rarely end up winning the battle of public opinion, the NNU has made itself an advocate for patients faced with the exigencies of care management (the advent of managerial tools in the health sector), and engages in a high level of activism that does not necessarily take the form of strikes. The NNU focuses not on wage demands, but on nurses' working conditions (which does not mean that its actions have no impact on wages) and ultimately in their criticality for patients' health. In particular, it seeks to establish a nurse-to-patient ratio. To this end it relies on works of epidemiology that indicate a strong correlation between the quality of hospitals and this ratio – a result that is largely intuitive for US citizens.

The NNU has its origins in a decision by the California Nursing Association, which now forms the biggest state union of nurses. In 1995, this association separated from the professional organization – the American Nursing Association – to constitute itself as a trade union and act more aggressively, while abandoning a corporatist logic and joining the American Federation of Labor and Congress of Industrial Organizations. At the beginning of 2004, after a campaign to make representatives and public opinion aware of the issues, Californian nurses secured legislation fixing the number of patients under supervision by one nurse at five (instead of the previous six). In the autumn, however, the governor of California, Arnold Schwarzenegger, decided to abolish this new norm, arguing that hospitals could not find sufficient staff and were being forced to shut services down. Faced with discontent from nurses, he asserted in virile fashion, 'I kick their butt', accusing them of corporatism.[1] Rose Ann DeMoro, then the leader of the California Nursing Association, went into battle, obtaining a court order suspending the governor's decision. Ten months later hospitals conformed, no service closed or reduced its activity, and patient satisfaction subsequently increased. The Terminator threw in the towel in late 2005.

The NNU's sphere of influence extends far beyond California, but it has not as yet conquered all workplaces or US states. We can estimate that it federates nearly 3 per cent of nurses in Alabama, 10 per cent in Maine, but at least one-quarter in Massachusetts, and more than 40 per cent in Hawaii.[2] The NNU above all presents itself as the defender of patients and working conditions. However, simply by dint of establishing a balance of power, the union is able to obtain a pay premium for nurses. By osmosis, other staff beyond the patrician body of doctors benefit from it: biologists and pharmacists. The graphics in Figure 6.2 indicate a 5 to 6 per cent increase in nurses' wages with a 10 per cent rate of unionization in the NNU within a state; this rate is lower, but still significant, for care assistants, whose potential gain is in the order of 1.5 per cent.[3]

---

1   Adam Tanner, 'Schwarzenegger Ends Fight with California Nurses', Reuters, 11 November 2005.
2   US trade unions are obliged to provide the Labor Department with a precise description of their finances and number of members. The Office of Labor Management Standards collects these union reports. Posted online, they make it possible to calculate the proportion of employed nurses belonging to one of the NNU's state unions. However, the reports may be incomplete or out of date, only making it possible to estimate a rate for half the states of the Union.
3   This elasticity is higher than that obtained by microeconomic work on the effect of the unionization of nurses on the basis of individual or institutional

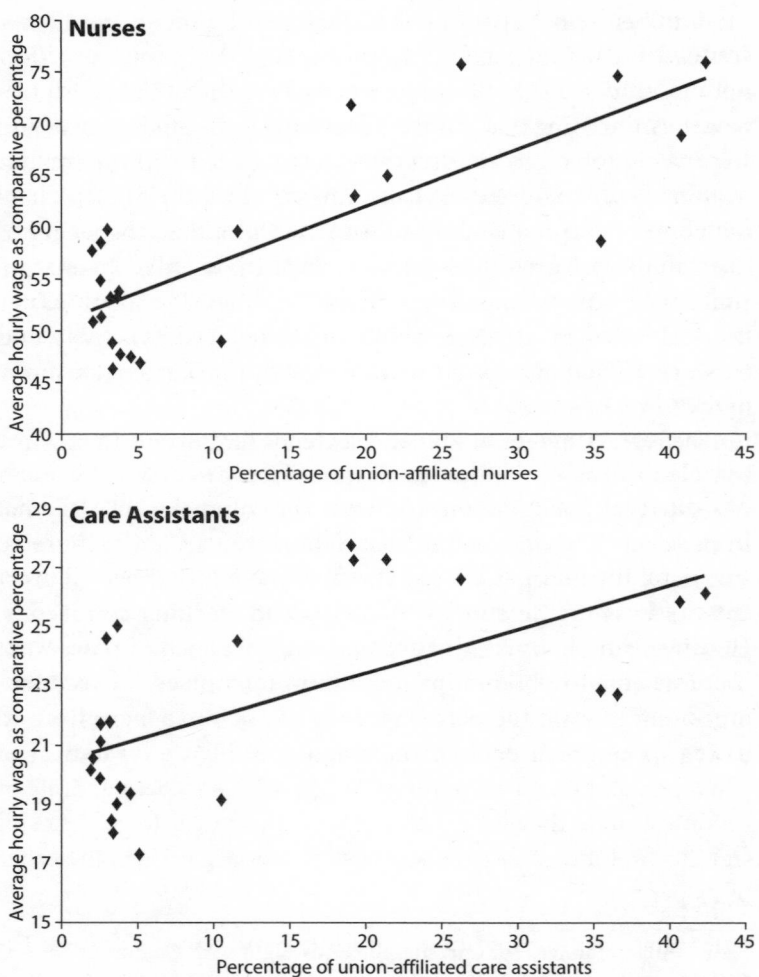

Figure 6.2 Correlation between Relative Wage of Nurses or Care Assistants and the Estimated Percentage of Nurses Affiliated with the NNU (24 US states, May 2014)

Sources: The percentage of unionized workers was calculated by dividing the number of members indicated by the union in the latest report available by the number of registered nurses estimated by the BLS in May 2014; the author pulled together the data for twenty-four states for which these reports were available from the Office of Labor Management Standards.

A propitious institutional environment and an innovative trade unionism, capable of marrying standard union practices with mobilization of public opinion and the alignment of criticality, show that the rearmament of labour is possible. However – in the absence of a renovated political space, at least – broad public support is only possible for causes where the public is the direct beneficiary. The Justice for Janitors movement, active for thirty years in the Anglophone world, has certainly achieved results on occasion, particularly on the working conditions of cleaning staff, but has failed to win over public opinion. More recently, hundreds of demonstrations organized throughout the United States against low pay in catering, and the blockading of some fast-food outlets on 15 April 2015, hardly registered beyond a fringe of the population. However, the organizers had precisely sought to enrol Middle America in their movement. The date of 15 April had not been selected by chance: Tax Day is the deadline for the payment of federal income tax. The argument was that half the employees in fast food can only survive thanks to benefits financed by taxes. In other words, citizens had every interest in supporting wage increases. In a boomerang effect, it was the restaurant owners' argument – that wage rises would have a knock-on effect on prices, directly hitting the customer's purse – that prevailed.[1]

A Localized Return of Class Struggle

Other shoots of trade unionism are now appearing, with strategies that for the time being are local and do not rely on the uncertain lever of public opinion. They involve targeted attacks

---

data. However, it is consistent with a 'fear' effect suggested by the literature: confronted with trade-union momentum in a state, non-unionized structures agree preventive wage increases. See, for example, Christopher Coombs, Robert Newman, Richard Cebula and Mary White, 'The Bargaining Power of Health Care Unions and Union Wage Premiums of Registered Nurses', *Journal of Labor Research* 36: 4 (2015).

1   Neither argument is strong: a wage increase may translate into reduced profit margins and have little impact on the requirements for financing benefits.

to demonstrate the criticality of an occupation, and thus recover a real but still miniscule share of their rent. In fact, a growing share of rents is dependent on the labour of the many, in particular in essential support roles (maintenance, gardening, and so on); rents are not necessarily appropriated by their direct employer, but often by the contractor further up. The agglomeration of productive activities, especially in clusters, concentrates this dependency in confined spaces. This configuration is now exposing capitalism to action based on the criticality of these workers' tasks, echoing the strategies of corporations. Industrial organization thus rediscovers one of the characteristics that favoured the emergence of working-class trade unionism: the blockading of a mine or factory made it possible to inflict significant losses.

Let us take a closer look at this through two examples of this phenomenon that show how subcontracted, poorly treated, invisible workers have mobilized: room attendants in the Parisian luxury hotels of the Golden Triangle, on one hand, and the support staff serving Silicon Valley giants, on the other. In both cases, the workers are under the thumb of monopsonies realizing fat profit margins, with subcontracting companies as a buffer; and in both cases, the workers, who are at the very bottom of the hierarchy of wages and working conditions, are shadowy figures in direct daily contact with social groups of winners.

The awakening of room attendants in the Golden Triangle

Paris, September 2013. A strange trade-union link-up has occurred among the teams of room attendants and valets employed by a specialist subcontractor and working at the Park Hyatt, Vendôme – a luxury hotel located on the rue de la Paix, at the very heart of the Golden Triangle. The subcontracted workers are members of the Confédération Générale du Travail (CGT) – the second-largest union in France – and the Confédération Nationale du Travail, a small anarcho-leftist trade union. Most of the room attendants are foreign. Their wages are very low and their work, at a pace worthy of *Modern Times*, nevertheless imposes strict quality demands.

Because the subcontracting firm works for numerous hotels, it can easily shift bolshie elements to another hotel without risking a case at an industrial tribunal. So the room attendants took their employer and Hyatt by surprise: they went on strike at a crucial time for Paris's luxury hotels, the days in late September and early October when it hosts Fashion Week, one of the hottest tickets in the industry.

The strikers very rapidly obtained the equivalent of a thirteenth month of pay, a re-evaluation of their qualifications within the branch collective agreement, the introduction of lunch vouchers, and restrictions on very irregular part-time work. Above all, they broke the fetter of the mobility clause. An employee paid by a subcontractor, and made available for more than twelve months on the site of a different enterprise, can choose to vote – and hence be elected – during workplace elections either at her direct employer or at the contracting party.[1] The room attendants and their colleagues chose to vote at Hyatt in autumn 2013. In September 2014, they were able to recommence the action while this time holding a position at the hotel. The potential loss to the establishment – the criticality – far exceeded the revenue associated with Fashion Week. The result was that management made new pay concessions, and work demands were reduced by increasing the time allotted for servicing rooms and suites by 10 per cent.[2] Their colleagues at Hyatt Madeleine, a few streets from the Vendôme, who were also on strike, won a similar agreement.

Also in autumn 2014, after a month-long strike, the Royal Monceau – another luxury hotel in the Champs-Élysées quarter, belonging to a Qatari fund that employed its own floor and kitchen staff – agreed in part to the CGT's demands. At the end of 2015, the subcontracted workers at the Park Hyatt suddenly

---

1 This is a recent provision of the French Labour Code introduced in 2008 in a law to modernize social dialogue, itself the result of the shared position of the two main French trade unions: the CFDT, privileged partner of governments (right- and left-wing alike) in France, and the CGT.

2 The 2014 agreement containing a reminder of the 2013 agreement is available at commerce.cgt.fr.

initiated industrial action and secured new benefits. They went back on strike in late September 2018, demanding their integration into the hotel's personnel. Despite an evacuation by the police in October, the strike continued, and negotiations were opened in mid November, a few days before the Champs-Élysées district became the scene of a confrontation between the Yellow Vests and the forces of law and order.

The spatial concentration of these actions is explained by a contagion effect and the size of the rents extracted by luxury tourism operators in the Golden Triangle. The motivation of the workforce probably also has its source in the vertigo that some employees must experience when faced with (often idle) clients from the world's wealthiest families.

Coach drivers confronting the giants of Silicon Valley

Silicon Valley, 2013. The giants of Web 2.0, mobility and biotech, are in a permanent state of development, and are always hiring inventors and engineers aplenty. Such is the strain on the housing market in the Valley that the companies – Facebook, Yahoo!, Google, and so on – have decided to organize private coach lines for the collaborators they cosset. The latter can thus reach their campus directly after a series of stops, particularly in San Francisco Bay. Facebook has a fleet of around seventy coaches, Google 200, and so forth. These coaches are comfortable and superequipped – air conditioning, Internet connection, and so on. But their drivers, employed by subcontractors, have not received any of the benefits offered to employees by the giants. Thousands of highly paid employees find themselves on campuses with optimal working conditions for expressing their 'creativity'; campuses that operate thanks to armies of small staffs – cooks, cleaners, janitors, and so on – who are, of course, subcontracted, and who have to find their own means of transport to their campus.

The sudden appearance of these coaches has caused urban change. New districts of San Francisco and Berkeley are undergoing accelerated gentrification, with significant rises in prices, particularly rents, near the coach stops. In addition, these stops are commonly used by the general public. The new traffic therefore creates delays, particularly on school routes. The local population demonstrates and sometimes blocks these coaches. The tech giants climb down in order to prevent their virtuous image being harmed, paying a modest fee to use the stops; Google even decides to pay several million dollars for school transport.

But the coach drivers remain invisible. This is a feature of the job, which is often isolated and invisible among a crowd of passengers. They are poorly remunerated because they are paid by the hour on a part-time basis. In fact, they only drive two to three hours on the journey out in the morning and then two to three hours again on the return trip in the evening, when the traffic is heavier. They get up at 5 a.m. and spend long, unpaid hours waiting in their vehicles during the day in order to return home in the evening.

In autumn 2014, one of the most powerful US trade unions, with 1.4 million members – the Teamsters – went on the offensive. In a few months, it succeeded in unionizing the drivers working for the subcontractors, among others those of Facebook, Apple, eBay and Genentech. A strike by these drivers, however short, would occasion considerable losses for these companies – potentially amounting to more than a century's worth of driver's wages. As a result, negotiations were started that concluded with agreements on pay rises. Google even decided to pre-empt developments. In addition to access during waiting hours to facilities (such as free gym halls) reserved for googlers (Google's direct employees), the drivers working through its five subcontractors obtained wage increases of 20 to 35 per cent, 80 per cent coverage of health costs for their family, and a savings plan for a personal pension – the so-called 401(k). The Teamsters are also seeking to win other occupations involving invisible workers with high criticality in Silicon Valley. Thus, in August 2015 it managed to unionize the subcontracted staff responsible for Genentech's waste management – a high-criticality activity in a biotech subsidiary of the Roche group. At the same time, under the pressure of another trade union, the SEIU United Service Workers West,

Apple decided in March 2015 to bring previously subcontracted security staff in-house.

Since then, the action has continued and become coordinated. Trade unions, community associations and religious leaders launched a united campaign – the 'Silicon Valley Rising' – to inspire the tech industry to create an inclusive middle class. The advances are secured one by one, but they are non-stop. Thus, in summer 2018 the SEIU obtained a collective agreement including paid holidays and health benefits for the 3,000 security staff of four major subcontractors of large Silicon Valley companies, including Facebook and Google, while the Teamsters achieved a significant wage increase for 600 subcontracted drivers transporting the employees of Tesla, Twitter and Electronic Arts.

The Teamsters also mobilized on the legal front. They won a victory at the National Labor Relations Board (NLRB) on 27 August 2015, despite the powerful mobilization of the bosses' lobbies. The status of co-employer was relaxed in order to be more easily identified. Thus, the collaborators of a subcontractor, or temps working exclusively for a contracting party, would have the latter as a co-employer. Similarly, the employees of a franchisee would theoretically have the franchiser as co-employer. A McDonald's team in a franchised restaurant would be recognized as co-employed by the McDonald's parent company, not only as employees of the restaurant. This would enable a majority trade union to negotiate with one or the other co-employer, or indeed with both; the contracting party or franchiser would no longer be able to shelter behind its subcontractor or franchisee. Once the new arrangement was in place, the Trump administration mobilized against this interpretation and, in the end, a majority of the NLRB decided in late 2018 to backtrack on its jurisprudence.

Wage-earners and platforms: the counter-attack

The business models of platforms for private drivers, bike deliveries, and concierge services for flats for travellers (a more attractive vocabulary is flat 'sitter' or 'carer') are still based on self-employment. This characterization has given rise to legal battles throughout the world, waged indirectly by corporations of artisans and employee trade unions, and directly by the 'jobbers' or platform workers themselves. The first of these battles were fought in the Californian cradle of the gig economy. Their main objective was recognition of the subordination involved in the work relationship, and hence its basic character as waged employment. Such is the stream of legal decisions and reversals that I shall not attempt a synthesis here. Moreover, the struggle goes beyond the legal terrain. Thus, Deliveroo or Uber Eats couriers organized strikes and even blockades in Belgium, France and the UK in 2018 and 2019.

History even suggests that the platforms, far from signalling the end of the wage-earning class, may form the basis for a revival of collective mobilizations. The simultaneous emergence of networks and platforms for so-called two-sided markets offering personalized services and goods produced by self-employed workers, all in the context of globalization, was already observed in the second half of the nineteenth century. Thus, in Haussmann's Paris, we find the emergence of urban transport networks and, at their hubs, large stores that served as intermediaries for myriad contractors – in other words, self-employed workers. Among them were those nicknamed *midinettes* – young girls in tailoring working for fashion houses that clothed the Parisian bourgeoisie, as well as foreign bourgeois passing through the city from Europe and North America. *Midinette* is a contraction of *midi* (*le Midi*, or south of France, also meaning noon) and *dinette* (light meal), because these workers often hailed from the south and went at midday with their lunch baskets to the parks of Paris, where they rubbed shoulders with the bourgeois whom they clothed. The painting by Renoir, *Les Parapluies* (1885) – alternately displayed at the Dublin City Gallery, also known as the Hugh Lane Gallery, and the National Gallery in London – is an illustration of this cohabitation: in the foreground a bareheaded *midinette*, elegant in her plain black clothes, surrounded by bourgeois – women, men, children – in more refined apparel. As Claude Didry shows, alongside the labour movement, the *midinettes'* mobilization over several decades, including during the First World War, enabled them to wrest the very first collective agreements that form the basis of the structuration of the wage-earning class in France.[1]

An organizational argument can also be invoked to project a possible future for platform workers far removed from a world of freelances.[2] A platform's capital is its technology, its database, its reputation and – most critically – the reputation of those who work through it. The latter are often graded and assessed by customer comments. A conflict of property law might crystallize around these comments: Do they belong to the platform, the worker who has been graded, or the customer? If a self-employed platform worker has built a reputation on platform A, and wishes to leave and set up on platform B, the non-transferability of comments will be a major obstacle to her mobility. If the platform – or law – does not permit transferability, she will become dependent on the platform regardless of whether she is characterized as employed; and it will no longer be able to refer to her as freelance. If transferability is established, then the value will shift from platform to worker, creating competition between platforms to recruit the best workers. The best option for platforms might then be to ensure the stability of their critical workforce, and retrieve full ownership of the comments by putting workers on the payroll.

Robots and Artificial Intelligence: The Fear Trap

Today, artificial intelligence (AI) feeds off human labour for its learning process; but analyses are alerting us to an increasing

---

1   Claude Didry, 'Les midinettes, avant-garde oubliée du prolétariat', *L'Homme & la Société* 189–190: 3 (2018).

2   These arguments are less pertinent in the case of the global labour market of micro-jobbing platforms (identification of images, verification of keywords, writing comments on forums, and so on) of the Amazon Mechanical Turk variety.

shortage of work with the irruption of a new industrial revolution of which robots and artificial intelligence are the vehicles.[1]

The prospect of a revival of labour would then be illusory: the warehouse workers at Amazon or the drivers of private-hire cars on the platforms, like those of the Silicon Valley coaches, can always mobilize, but they will soon disappear.

A document by the Oxford academics Carl Frey and Michael Osborne, predicting the replacement by machines of the jobs of around half of workers in the advanced countries, has had a big impact, provoking a lively debate since its publication.[2] In every instance, history teaches us that predictions about technology's impact on employment have most often proved wrong. And this is not the first time automation has inspired fears about the disappearance of jobs. Ten years after the notion of AI was invented, in 1956, a report by the National Commission on Technology, Automation, and Economic Progress was already expressing concern, while highlighting the opportunities afforded by such forms of technology.[3]

If we confine ourselves to projections by robotics manufacturers for the short and medium term, the extension of the use of robots in manufacturing will continue at a constant pace. In other sectors, by contrast, robotics and AI will together experience

---

1   This section adapts elements of two of my columns in *Le Monde*.

2   A working document of 2013 published in a journal four years later: 'The Future of Employment: How Susceptible Are Jobs to Computerisation?', *Technological Forecasting and Change* 114 (C) (2017).

3   'It is easy to oversimplify the course of history; yet if there is one predominant factor underlying current social change, it is surely the advancement of technology ... The technological advances which may be possible in the future will come not only from machines, but from what has been called "intellectual technology", the application of new computer-using techniques ... In the new technology, machines and automated processes will do the routine and mechanical work ... the medical system of the United States faces critical problems ... More could be done with larger information systems. Regional health computer centers could provide medical record storage for perhaps 12 to 20 million people and give hospitals and doctors in an area access to the computer's diagnostic.'

a growth spurt, though from a very low starting-point. Thus, throughout the world, the famous robot receptionists will at most number in the tens of thousands in 2022. Taking SAE International as a benchmark, the advent of completely autonomous vehicles represents the fifth stage of a process that has not yet really reached its third stage, not to mention the various legal insurance and ethical obstacles presented by this technology. In the medical domain, where investment is most massive, the mission of very costly robots is not to replace human beings, but to improve their productivity at a time when the training of new professionals is not keeping up with expanding needs.

More generally, in several countries automation technologies are regarded as a solution to demographic decline and the future workforce requirements that will be created by adapting to climate change and the energy transition. This is true in Germany, where net annual immigration of 400,000 would be required for the next two decades to offset the natural decline in the working population. Recent works have formalized a demographic determinism confirmed by empirical evidence. Thus, Ana Abeliansky and Klaus Prettner find a strong positive correlation between demographic decline and the use of industrial robots in a large sample of countries.[1]

At the same time, automation's capacity to establish itself beyond the standardized, mechanized, industrial universe has been met with a challenge. The case of Japan is illuminating. A touchstone country for fifty years, Japan has recently embarked on a massive robotics project. It is endeavouring both to maintain its leadership by capitalizing on the marriage between robotics, AI and IOT (the 'Internet of things') and to respond with these technologies to its demographic winter while preserving the Japanese nation: unlike an immigrant, perhaps a 'nipponized' robot will be able to express itself in fluent Japanese, and, in the case of humanoid robots, to assume the idealized features of a Japanese

---

1   Ana Abeliansky and Klaus Prettner, 'Working Paper: Automation and Demographic Change', Cege Discussion Papers no. 310 (2017).

woman or man.[1] The partial U-turn on immigration by the Conservative government of Shinzo Abe in November 2018 highlights the limits of its plan: it is arranging for the entry of foreign workers into catering, construction and care services.

The key scientific question thus tends to shift: it now concerns not so much knowing the pace at which technology is going to replace us as understanding why its employment is slipping.[2] Unsuitability for much more complex and unpredictable situations? Rejection of a kind of infantilization of users? A refusal to see human relationships disappear?

But the idea of a rapid transformation driven by AI remains present in public debate. Actors in advanced technologies have a twofold interest in maintaining it. The first relates purely to business and shareholding: their techno-optimistic discourses open up sizeable markets for them, pushing businesses into costly investments, and maintains the value of their shares.

The second is much more political. The discourse on employment promoted by Elon Musk and Mark Zuckerberg, which in this instance is techno-pessimistic, is accompanied by a political solution presented as progressive: the introduction of a universal basic income. The platform of the Democratic Party in California adopted this proposal in 2018: 'We support efforts to enact programs, such as a guaranteed government jobs program and a universal basic income'. This echoes the recommendations of the National Commission half a century earlier: '(1) a program of public-service employment in which the government would be an "employer of last resort" of hard-core unemployed, (2) an income floor to guarantee the economic security of families'. One of the distinguished members of the Commission was Thomas J. Watson, CEO of IBM (and the Democrat Jimmy Carter's future ambassador to the Soviet Union).[3]

---

1   Jennifer Robertson, *Robo Sapiens Japanicus: Robots, Gender, Family and the Japanese Nation* (Oakland: University of California Press, 2018).

2   See Philippe Askenazy and Francis Bach, 'IA et emploi: une menace artificielle', *Pouvoirs* 170 (2019).

3   Watson is currently the name of IBM's Artificial Intelligence programme.

The archaeology of the idea of basic income in Europe, and its re-emergence, provide the analytical key to the support it enjoys among the giants of Silicon Valley.[1] In 1984, the neoliberal revolution was only in its early stages. In Belgium, a collective led by Philippe Van Parijs, professor at Louvain University, sought not to challenge it, but to complete it by offering a substitute for most existing social-security arrangements. With the universal benefit, Van Parijs won the competition of the King Baudouin Foundation on the future of work. An international network was to emerge from this kernel, with its first conference outside Belgium in 1990 in Florence, where Van Parijs taught at the European University Institute.

From a neoliberal perspective, basic income is the twin of flat tax: equal rights; primacy of individual responsibility; a simple system, and hence minimal state; perpetuation of the social order. If, especially in a US context, it might seem more attractive than meagre social rights, it will nonetheless lead to the disappearance of parts of social security and some benefits.[2] While basic income is supposed to strengthen the individual employee's bargaining power, it would above all make it possible to dispense with collective representation of workers. By offering a guaranteed means of obtaining financing, it would facilitate the stimulation of entrepreneurship. But it would not shield a bankrupt self-employed person from poverty, since she would have to use her universal benefit to pay off her debts. The benefit then turns into surety for the banks.

This explains why, when universal income was a serious option on the Belgian political agenda at the start of the century, the main trade-union organizations opposed it. It also highlights a minimal coherence in the coalition that arrived in power in Italy in 2018: it contains the League, supporter of the flat tax, and the Five Star

---

1   See, for example, the short book by Mateo Alaluf, *L'allocation universelle* (Brussels: Editions Couleur Livres, 2014).

2   Interestingly, Andrew Yang, an entrepreneur candidate in the 2020 Democrat presidential primary, proposed a universal basic income (12,000 dollars per annum) in 2019. However, its recipients would lose government benefits such as the Supplemental Nutrition Assistance Program.

movement, favourable to a basic income; the two parties also coincide in their detestation of trade unions. Finally, this accounts for the interest of Silicon Valley's billionaires, who clearly perceive the threat represented by a revival of the world of labour and the attractiveness of having self-employed workers at their disposal.

What Kind of Non-Pragmatic Politics?

A different political option is to assist a radical renewal in the mobilization of workers. From victories to defeats, one of the objectives of an active trade unionism is (to adopt neoclassical terminology) to transform outsiders into insiders. The weapon of the law is increasingly mobilized, but actions targeted on the heart of the capitalist machine are still limited today. As in the social-democratic parties, neoliberal fables inform the thinking of many wage-earners' trade unions in the advanced economies. However, the trade-union world could rapidly adopt a concentric strategy, starting with systematic action in the occupations and sectors with the highest criticality, whether organizational or reputational in origin. Reflection on such a strategy goes well beyond the scope of this book. However, we may note the under-utilization of the tools of the digital revolution. Social networks have proved their power in the Arab revolutions, as in the emergence of new political forces in Europe or of the Yellow Vests in France. In the sphere of work, they can facilitate an experience of sharing, with the simultaneous national or international mobilization of sites of the same enterprise. Still very marginal, crowdfunding has already been mobilized to finance strike funds and local structures of network access for workers.

Obviously, these mobilizations of the world of labour and efforts to accumulate new knowledge of labour run counter to conservative and neoliberal ideologies. What might a novel political positioning of social democracy or American liberalism consist in? We need to distinguish between the level of discourse and principles and that of public policy.

Going beyond useful measures country by country, it would, in the first instance, involve ensuring a space for collective mobilization that responds to changes in the bonds of subordination and in the organization of workplaces.[1] In effect, trade-union freedom faces two obstacles: on one hand, the phenomenon of subcontracting, temping or franchising, which concentrates groups of social losers; on the other, in certain activities the multiplicity of establishments of the same enterprise or group.

The first obstacle means the direct employer is often under the thumb of the purchaser or franchiser, who employs precisely this mode of organization of production to optimize his rents.[2] This is not always the case. For example, in large retailers, we find super-franchises – that is, (families of) owners of a large number of sales points in franchises generating considerable profits. This type of set-up is not always identifiable by statisticians, which implies a probable underestimate of the influence of monopsony in certain sectors.

Securing the extension of the notion of co-employer would enable the subcontracted and other franchised elements to confront directly those who determine their subordination. Depending on each country's institutions, these workers could form trade-union branches to negotiate with the pool of employers, take part and be elected in workplace elections, and join the health and safety committees of the various employers. The notion of co-employer might even be extended to businesses employing freelances who are in fact economically dependent on those firms, or largely subordinate to them.

1   Measures within any given country largely depend on the initial state of labour law or social relations. For example, in the United States abolition of employers' ability to replace a striker with a hire on a permanent contract was a commitment of Obama's campaign that never bore fruit.

2   Alan B. Krueger and Orley Ashenfelter, 'Theory and Evidence on Employer Collusion in the Franchise Sector', IZA DP no. 11672 (2018), reports the frequent presence in chains like McDonald's and Burger King in the United States of the franchise clause 'no poaching of workers agreements' – that is, clauses of non-competition between franchises in recruiting employees.

Even when it is clear who the employer is, the multiplicity of establishments and subsidiaries splinters the capacity for collective mobilization. Large retailers are emblematic: Walmart has 11,000 stores in the world; Carrefour has 5,600 shops in France and 1,000 in Italy; Lidl has 3,200 in Germany; Mercadona has 1,600 in Spain – and so on. Legally securing digital spaces of interaction between the employees of physically scattered entities on their working conditions, management or pay within the enterprise or group, is one possible way of guaranteeing freedom of collective mobilization against the employer.

But the first imperative is political. We need to abandon the sterile debate dominated by pragmatism or the register of fear. The pursuit of competitiveness has become macroeconomically and ecologically deadly: seemingly victorious, conservatives and neoliberals face a contradiction in their economic policy offer. Above all: inequalities are not natural, everyone's contribution to the economic and social system must be recognized, and a collective surge by labour is possible. In the spirit of the insider/outsider theory, reforms for the individualization and flexibilization of the labour market aim to eliminate the insiders but actually weaken the position of the poorly paid and discriminated workers. By contrast, the path I propose would promote a society of insiders.

The obvious political trap would be to succumb to other forms of pragmatism. On both sides of the Atlantic, the construction of a Green New Deal provides an illustration of this. Let us take its archetype – the resolution presented by several representatives, most prominently Alexandria Ocasio-Cortez, to the US Congress on 7 February 2019. Taken one by one, the proposals are ambitious and seek to outline an inclusive economy tackling ecological issues. But the construction of the draft is intended to be pragmatic: it starts out from the climate crisis, treating it as a matter of consensus because it is firmly rooted in science, and hence capable of attracting an electoral majority. Then it advocates the state as employer of last resort for the victims of the requisite closure of polluting and carbon-emitting activities, and calls for stronger collective rights, particularly trade-union rights, in the new activities of the energy transition. Finally, to finance this industrial and social transition, the draft proposes taxing the wealthiest. Rather than confront the current capitalist social order, Green New Deals seek to circumvent it (while recycling a tax proposal the obstacles to which I have highlighted). In so doing, they risk attracting neither basically politicized popular classes, as indicated by budding social struggles, nor environmentalists, who might just as well be persuaded by a greenwashed neoliberalism.

By contrast, a non-pragmatic offer challenging the socioeconomic order might achieve this coalition. It would affirm that bringing down this order is a necessary condition for resolving the social and climate crises. In and of themselves, inequalities generate overconsumption and mal-consumption that are damaging the planet. In and of themselves, propertarianism, domination and the commodification of the public are incompatible with the preservation of global environmental public goods.

7

Weakening the Hand of Property

Propertarianism rules unchallenged. The extension of the sphere of property and real estate's power to absorb agglomeration benefits are trump cards in the hands of present-day capitalists. The property right has become all the more absolute in that collective ownership of the means of production – an alternative form of ownership – has been swept away by history. Exclusive ownership of knowledge now seems natural.

History seems to have been wiped from people's memories. It has been forgotten that the patentability of medicines went through many twists and turns from the start of the industrial era until the second half of the twentieth century.[1] Confronted with chemists and the original pharmaceutical industrial enterprises redeeming the fixed costs of their investments, dispensary pharmacists highlighted the risks to patients and public health of overly expensive medicines supplied by monopolies protected by patents. Thus, in France a law of 5 July 1844 proscribed the patentability of 'pharmaceutical compounds or remedies of any

---

1 Jean-Paul Gaudillière, 'L'industrialisation du médicament: une histoire de pratiques entre sciences, techniques, droit et médecine', *Gesnerus: Swiss Journal of the History of Medicine and Sciences* 64: 1–2 (2007). See also Benjamin Coriat, ed., *Le Retour des communs* (Paris: Les Liens qui libèrent, 2015).

kind'. In the major European producer countries, it was only after the Second World War that patentability began to become fully established. In France, medicines only joined common patent law very belatedly, in 1969, after strong pressure from the ministry of economy, which was already arguing for the need for European convergence.

The Contradictions of the Voter

Challenging propertarianism today is not easy. Indeed, it has a strong electoral base: the majority of voters in most of the advanced countries are homeowners. This propertarianism plunges citizens into contradictions found in varying degrees throughout the advanced economies.

An initial contradiction concerns the taxability of capital – an estate or income from an estate. The vast majority of owner-occupiers would gain from redistributive taxation on estates, accompanied by systems of exemptions covering small or even medium estates. It would make it possible to lower other contributions or finance public goods from which they would benefit. However, the implementation of such taxation collides with the fear of small property owners, whipped up by supporters of propertarianism – the fear of the state ultimately getting its hands on their estate, 'fruit of a lifetime's work'. A society of small property owners neuters political strategies based on denouncing inequalities and calling for 'tax revolutions'. It provides a form of democratic protection to big estates.

Reverence for property creates a second contradiction, involving the world of business. On the one hand, dismissing workers in order to enhance shareholder value, like recourse to relocation, scandalizes public opinion. On the other, shareholder value itself is not called into question: it is accepted that an enterprise has the overriding objective of satisfying its shareholding owners. The conception of the 'modern' corporation as the fruit of a compromise between stakeholders – employers, employees, subcontractors – that prevailed after the New Deal seems to have been forgotten.[1] The co-determination model of governance does not escape this reverence:[2] trade-union representatives sitting on boards of directors swap guarantees of industrial peace, silence on the fate of subcontractors and maximization of profits with dividends for a stable core of employees. According to the national accounts of the major advanced economies, it is in Germany, homeland of co-determination, that capital's share in the value-added of non-financial companies increased most at the start of the century: it rose sharply from 39 per cent in 2000 to nearly 47 per cent in 2007, dropped back during the crisis, and then settled at a still high level of around 42 per cent.[3] It is also in Germany that an explosion of poverty in work was to be seen, exceeding 20 per cent of workers until the minimum wage was introduced. The prevalent view of the business orientated towards shareholders is, in fact, an obstacle to the strengthening of labour. But it is much easier to overcome than the obstacle confronting fiscal strategies for the secondary distribution of income.

The Shadowy Benefits of Ownership

Weakening political propertarianism is therefore indispensable from the standpoint of a policy of income distribution. How can we backtrack on the construction of a society of small property owners? Before exploring various paths, we have to answer those who argue that this model of society enhances social cohesion and democratic participation.

---

1   See Adolf Berle and Gardiner Means, *The Modern Corporation and Private Property* (New York: Macmillan, 1932).

2   In corporate governance, co-determination is the practice of workers having the right to vote for representatives on the board of directors of their company; in Germany, this scheme is required by law in large firms.

3   Eurostat annual national accounts – profit share of non-financial corporations TEC00100 – consulted 2 August 2019. Provisional quarterly statistics suggest that this share has eroded during 2019.

This current of thought, or rather these currents, whose roots lie in the nineteenth century, have an enduring power. For example, for Frédéric Le Play, 'The more I study the social problem, the more convinced I am that the first degree of well-being does not consist in extending physical satisfactions, but in creating the moral enjoyment of property.'[1] An enormous international, trans-disciplinary contemporary literature– in law, philosophy, political science, sociology, economics – confirms this view.[2] To be an owner-occupier supposedly brings benefits for individuals and positive externalities for society. These potential externalities justify the arrangements, particularly tax provisions, that incentivize ownership in most OECD countries.

Citizenship, individual satisfaction and financial insurance

Supporters of homeownership advance three types of argument, often in some kind of combination: better citizenship, greater individual satisfaction, and financial insurance for households.

Citizenship is supposedly improved by two mechanisms: the transformative role of ownership and its character as an investment. Becoming a property owner is said to transform the

---

1   Louis Baudin, *Frédéric Le Play. Textes choisis* (Paris: Dalloz, 1947). Le Play proceeds in the same text to analyse the industrial revolution in England: 'I have always recognized, in contrast, that the prior need for comfort closes off to the English worker and his descendants the path leading to property. The very practice of England justifies the principle I have just established regarding the close link that always obtains among the lower classes between the simplicity of existence and the route to property' (pp. 157–8 of the electronic version published on the digital library 'Les classiques de sciences sociales' of the University of Québec at Chicoutimi, at classiques.uqac.ca.

2   For an accessible but comprehensive review of the arguments, see Stephanie M. Stern, 'Reassessing the Citizen Virtues of Homeownership', *Columbia Law Review* 111: 4 (April 2011). It should be noted that authors can endorse some arguments and refute others. Thus, Joseph Stiglitz, *The Price of Inequality* (New York: W.W. Norton, 2012) underlines the impact of home-ownership on citizenship, while highlighting the financial risks of ownership for those on the lowest incomes.

individual into an autonomous member of a local community. This encourages her to integrate more with her neighbours and to become involved in community associations or public affairs. Becoming an owner also makes the individual respectful of property, and therefore diverts her from any kind of delinquency. From an economic point of view, investment in real estate is, by its very nature, prolonged and illiquid, with significant transaction costs. The long-term value of a property depends on the positive externalities of a pleasant neighbourhood, where everyone has an interest in maintaining their property. Consent to local taxation is far higher among owner-occupiers. In fact, taxation feeds investment in local public goods that enhance the occupant's immediate well-being and, above all, the value of private properties. This is particularly true of highly conspicuous projects such as the building of schools and sports facilities.

A second type of argument bears on the individual in her psychological sphere. Self-esteem is said to depend on achievements throughout life. Becoming a property owner marks a key stage in it, especially given that the statistical correlation between social status and being an owner-occupier enables the individual who enjoy homeownership not to change objective status, but to imagine that she is perceived differently within her milieus – family, neighbours, colleagues. As a result, owner-occupiers are more satisfied than tenants.

Finally, various economic arguments underscore the insurance represented by bricks and mortar. In the event of one of life's mishaps – loss of employment, in particular – housing, notwithstanding its non-liquidity, holds out the possibility of absorbing a major shock by selling. For smaller shocks, not being subject to the pressure of a rent makes it easier to adjust expenditure. Americans' aspiration to ownership goes back to the Great Depression of the 1930s. The maximum number of people accessing ownership should almost automatically reduce inequalities of wealth at the bottom of the pyramid.

The domination of pro-ownership arguments is such that, once again, history has been forgotten. In the 1970s the Scandinavian societies were presented as an alternative to a society of owner-occupiers.[1] A very large majority of householders in them were tenants. In return, social protection was generous and seen as everyone's capital. It was also the guarantor of a high degree of civic engagement and high individual and collective satisfaction in a relatively egalitarian society at ease with itself.

The transformation of the Scandinavian societies into societies of owner-occupiers in the intervening decades does not seem to have improved their functioning. Worse, they have not escaped the rise of extreme right-wing populist parties since the start of the century (the True Finns, the Danish People's Party, the Norwegian Progress Party, the Swedish Democrats). In fact, the contradictions articulated by property-owning voters everywhere serve as a breeding-ground for forms of populism, from the US Tea Party, via France's Rassemblement National and the Alternative für Deutschland, to Italy's Lega. Unlike the political families that dominated political life from the fall of the Berlin Wall to the Great Recession, right-wing populism helps voters escape their contradictions. They identify a third party as the culprit for their difficulties: in the first instance immigrants, but also those on welfare benefits, who are often identified with the former. In addition, immigrants can easily be accused of threating small individual properties – either directly through theft or damage, or on account of a fall in property values in areas where they have settled. Propertarianism and anti-immigrant populism are thus tending to coalesce in a bid to guarantee the capitalist order at the expense of the democratic order. Viktor Orbán's Hungary, where homeownership is above 85 per cent (compared, for example, to around 65 per cent in the United States), affords an illustration of this tendency.

---

1   See Jim Kennedy, *The Myth of Home Ownership* (London: Routledge, 1982).

Everyone in debt?

At the same time, the Great Recession spectacularly undermined the insurance argument for property ownership. The origin of the 2008 crisis is to be found in an instrument deployed on a massive scale by the financial sphere, with the approval of the public authorities, to enable everyone to accede to the American dream of ownership: subprime mortgages. Millions of households that had contracted these loans found themselves unable to repay them. The celebrated insurance turned into hell with the collapse of the housing bubble: eviction, descent into poverty, and so forth. Fairly similar cycles occurred in Europe, from Spain to Ireland. More than a decade later, these economies still bear the scars. The British began to run up excessive debt once again, while prices took off (until the Brexit vote), especially in Greater London. The Scandinavian countries, which hold the record for housing debt, are creating legitimate anxieties. Housing propertarianism has become a twofold threat – individual and economic.

Prior to the crisis, the economic insurance supposedly offered to those on low incomes by ownership had been challenged. For example, the right to buy introduced by Margaret Thatcher in the 1980s encouraged a large number of council house tenants to buy their homes. However, such investment did not always benefit from a favourable development in property prices, particularly the rise caused by gentrification. In fact, it involved often ghettoized areas without attractive public goods. Worse, these locations might be in areas of the old economy that had experienced sharp demographic decline, leaving the owner-occupier with a devalued or even unsaleable property.[1] Furthermore, properties in a collective or individual building regularly require major expenditure (replacing a roof, bringing a lift up to standard, and so on), which can plunge those on low incomes into considerable financial difficulties. The dream of everyone being an owner does not guarantee a more egalitarian society in terms of estates, especially in the mid-to-long term.

---

1   See Ray Forrest, Alan Murie and Peter Williams, *Home Ownership: Differentiation and Fragmentation* (London: Unwin Hyman, 1990).

Property against mobility?

Updating surveys on social behaviour and satisfaction has made it possible to test both arguments based on psychology and those based on civic engagement. The exercise is highly complex, because access to ownership is correlated with a large number of individual and household characteristics. In addition, reverse causalities are frequent: thus, a household that 'feels good' in a district or city (based on participation in the community and individual satisfaction) will want to settle there, which increases its inclination to purchase a property.

The results obtained by statistical work, although not wholly convergent, suggest two things. First, the deeper one goes, the more the complexity of ownership's potential impact is revealed. For example, in New Zealand it turns out that, while owners participate more in local elections, their satisfaction with the performance of local representatives is lower.[1] This indicates that being an owner increases expectations and brings disappointments, thus reducing community social capital.

Second, the correlations between homeownership and individual satisfaction or collective engagement – measured by numerous indicators such as charitable donations, participation in community associations, and so on – are relatively weak. They collapse when account is taken of duration of residence, which is much higher for owner-occupiers.

Various works in political economy stress that mobility is an important factor in the labour market. By contrast, people settling down is said to restrict job opportunities, and exposes them to an increased risk of unemployment in the event of the employment zone's decline (such as following closure of a large industrial factory). Scholars who promote the matching theory of the labour market are therefore rather hostile to ownership, at any rate prior to retirement age. The Great Recession offered a

---

1   Matthew Roskruge, Arthur Grimes, Philip McCann and Jacques Poot, 'Homeownership, Social Capital and Satisfaction with Local Government', *Urban Studies* 50: 12 (2013).

test bed for these theoretical hypotheses. However, at least in the short term the results do not suggest a massive impact on the risk of unemployment from being an owner-occupier in most of the countries studied, regardless of whether they were affected by the subprime crisis.[1]

On the other hand, over the long term a higher proportion of owner-occupiers in the United States seems to generate what are called 'negative externalities': statistically, doubling the percentage of owners in a state entails more than doubling the level of long-term unemployment.[2] Ownership is said to involve three problems: lower labour mobility, increased journey time to and from work, and reduced entrepreneurship. Furthermore, we may note that global cities generally have a proportion of tenants (particularly in private housing stock) far above that of the surrounding areas. For example, Paris is distinguished from the rest of France by a majority of tenants, high mobility – and a minority of car owners.

To conclude, the facts do not allow us to confer upon ownership the laurels of the positive externalities spotlighted by its advocates, including the lobbies of real-estate promoters and the financial sector.

Fewer Property Owners and More Affordable Housing

We may therefore renounce occupant propertarianism without undue concern – or, rather, reverse the movement of recent decades. Just as propertarianism became established step by step, such a turn can only be a long-term objective. However, we can immediately set out on new roads. Two can be explored in the immediate present: private housing stock for rent, and social

---

1   On Germany, for example, see Marco Caliendo, Anne C. Gielen and Robert Mahlstedt, 'Home-Ownership, Unemployed's Job Search Behavior and Post-Unemployment Outcomes', *Economics Letters* 137 (2015).

2   David Blanchflower and Andrew Oswald, 'Does High Home-Ownership Impair the Labor Market?', NBER Working Paper No. 19079 (2013).

housing stock. The first signifies that a minority of owners automatically receive (directly or via property companies) rents on housing and land. For the purposes of balanced allocation, the development of a social stock for rent is therefore a priority. Let us note immediately that opponents of state action in this area highlight the crowding out of the private rental sector: real estate being scarce, and the capacity for building new housing limited, public (or quasi-public) investment reduces the development of private stock, and hence makes it impossible to respond meaningfully to insufficient supply.[1] While these findings are open to discussion, in my approach they strengthen the path towards building up the public rental stock. The latter would in fact yield a double dividend, by often supplying affordable accommodation to people on low incomes and driving out rentier landlords (whether private individuals or property companies).

In every country, social housing covers a range of rents for different audiences. Varieties of accommodation may cohabit in the same joint-ownership property under rubrics that vary from one country to another, and which are eloquent in themselves, from 'highly social' via 'affordable' to 'intermediate'. To these we might add 'non-profit-making accommodation for specific groups', such as students. The aim is to cover a sufficiently broad population to ensure a form of social mix. In all countries, social housing benefits from provisions of direct or tax aid; but the scale of such arrangements varies greatly from one country to the next and, depending on policy options, they may be subject to significant alteration over time. Thus, France and the UK inherited a stock of affordable housing higher than 15 per cent of homes from the post–Second World War reconstruction, whereas it reached barely 2 per cent of the total housing stock in Spain.

Spain represents an extreme case of pro-homeownership policies. But all countries encourage homeownership for purposes of either occupation or renting. For example, in France multiple tax

---

1   For example, Michael D. Eriksen and Stuart S. Rosenthal, 'Crowd Out Effects of Place-Based Subsidized Rental Housing: New Evidence from the LIHTC Program', *Journal of Public Economics* 94: 11–12 (2010).

provisions, adorned with the names of various housing ministers, are regularly introduced in favour of landlords. Aside from these, anyone who buys a property can deduct from her tax base the main work done after purchase to enhance the property (apart from its extension), the interest on loans taken out for the purchase, and property taxes; purchase of a new property benefits from a reduced property-transfer fee, and so on. All tax-payers, including the biggest, benefit from these arrangements.

Backtracking on these arrangements, or curbing them, has the advantage of maintaining current owner-occupiers: the political risk to a government of mobilization of these voters is therefore limited. The associated fiscal leeway can enable an ambitious social-housing policy. Meanwhile, the liberation of public real estate can assist in the diversification of housing supply.

Here the policy initiated in France by Lionel Jospin's Socialist government in coalition with the Greens is rather advanced within the OECD, and is worth detailing. The law on solidarity and urban renewal (SRU) of 13 December 2000 set the objective of a floor of 20 per cent of social housing (including all categories, from municipal housing to workers' hostels) in most communes of more than 1,500 inhabitants in the Île-de-France, and of 3,500 in the provinces in an agglomeration experiencing demographic growth. A law of 2013 raised the rate for some communes to 25 per cent. Communes that do not introduce a plan to achieve these targets are penalized by deductions from their tax resources. The state can even appropriate land, and – since the 2014 ALUR law – buildings to construct social housing in the event of a commune's failure to do so. The ALUR law governing access to housing and urban renovation also introduced a new state tool: from imperatives of safety, hygiene and human dignity, the state or local authorities can intervene in degraded private co-owned properties to appropriate and acquire lots to initiate works with a plan for rehousing the occupants. In practice, use of these provisions is extremely rare – but it demonstrates the legal capacity of a state to encourage an alternative policy to that of universal property ownership.

Nevertheless, the development of social housing requires great vigilance in terms of governance. Two dimensions are especially critical. The first involves coordinating and directing resources to the various actors in social housing. Homes must be created where the needs are most crying, while avoiding urban segregation. Improvement in the flow of supply must be organized to facilitate tenants' occupational and familial mobility. The second dimension bears on the use of what, certainly on the face of it, are non-profit-making private bodies to take on social-housing projects; social housing is not synonymous with public housing. The presence of certain big players from the profit-making private sector in the management of such bodies indicates, moreover, that pursuit of rent is never far off. For example, one of the main HLM (council housing) operators in France – the Logement Français group – has as its major shareholder, with an 80 per cent stake, AXA, the premier global insurance company. This enables some actors to give themselves a social veneer when they are uninhibited participants in the management of their private stock. The combination of the roles of private landlord and social-housing property-management company makes it possible to receive rent on the second segment, even to create synergies in mixed ensembles – social–private, profitable–private – so as to maximize profits. Likewise, officially in order to finance new building, these bodies can sell to tenants, and one then lapses back into individual ownership and its attendant risks for those on low incomes.

Terminating Intangible Property

While the property right may retain a form of democratic immunity for some years to come, propertarianism in intangible things has probably reached a peak. The anti-patent arguments of the first half of the twentieth century have re-emerged, or been rediscovered. In his *The Great Divide*, Joseph Stiglitz analyses, for example, the impact of property rights in medicines and diagnostic tests on inequalities in the United States.[1] He stresses that these rights imperil the health of the great majority, allowing their holders to impose prohibitive prices that maximize their rents by relying on the most affluent patients.

The contribution of patentability to innovation is even discussed in so orthodox a review as the *Journal of Economic Perspectives*.[2] More significantly, the OECD is currently adopting arguments long invoked by specialists in the commons.[3] The organization even alludes to the 'tragedy of the anti-commons'. I have already referred to some of these arguments. There is now unanimity about the impact of the fragmentation and multiplication of rights in the context of a growth in products involving a large number of technologies. For example, in producing its mobile phones, Apple is obliged to use technologies under Samsung patents – and, conversely, Samsung uses Apple technologies in its products. Ultimately, the scramble for patents generates a confusion of the various parties' rights, and the risk of key patents being retained to block developments by competitors. This situation would constrain innovation and reinforce uncertainty; in fact, it translates into legal disputes that occasion considerable expense, exposing innovators to enormous financial penalties.

Big capital is split on this issue. The power of companies in the 'new economy' is largely based on intellectual property rights that can be immediately applied to a global market. Such is this power today that Google and Facebook can extend their activities to new sectors of the economy, from communications infrastructure via cars to health. The giants of the 'old economy' are therefore now pushing for differentiated intellectual property, retaining their privileges but limiting those of their putative competitors.

---

1   Joseph Stiglitz, *The Great Divide: Unequal Societies and What We Can Do about Them* (New York: W.W. Norton, 2015).

2   See Michele Boldrin and David K. Levine, 'The Case against Patents', *Journal of Economic Perspectives* 27: 1 (2013).

3   OECD, *The Future of Growth* (Paris: OECD, 2015).

This new awareness, and these new circumstances of inter-capitalist relations, are not yet capable of impelling significant alterations in property rights in intangible goods. Following the Lima agreement, concluded under OECD auspices in October 2015, governments have slowly initiated fiscal policies to restrict tax evasion by multinationals – especially when it is facilitated by the parking of income from royalties on intangible property or intangible services.[1] The European Commission is seeking to have the tax rulings (tax advantages negotiated by multinationals) practised in countries such as Luxembourg and the Netherlands recognized as illegal state aid. This will not reduce the scale of these players' primary rents, however. In addition, intensive industries in intangibles would be able to avoid the future environmental tax regimes that will one day germinate in the face of climate change.

Theories of the commons propose to circumvent the obstacle of the exclusive property right to discover a dynamic of innovation and avoid the constitution of monopoly rents. The archetype is free software, or the collaborative wikis where individuals coop-erate to construct and develop a 'common good'. But, beyond these cases, the various approaches of the commons have not yet demonstrated a capacity to exert any real influence – still less their sustainability in market economies.

Establishing new balances of power is another path. I shall take two examples that involve sums totalling hundreds of bil-lions of dollars. The first power relationship had already been recast in several European countries, but has been set aside in the Untied States with the election of Donald Trump. It involves health systems able to square up to the pharmacy and biotech-nology giants.

---

1   For example, Facebook paid only a little over €300,000 in tax in France in 2014. In fact, its French subsidiary declared a very low turnover. Adver-tising targeting French Internet users – the bulk of Facebook's business – is invoiced not from France, but Ireland, In 2019, Facebook still pays a ridiculous €6 million in tax.

Health systems confronting the pharmacy and biotechnology giants

In the United States in autumn 2015, a lively debate developed over pharmaceutical industry rents, under the influence of the candidates for the Democratic nomination. The United States has no agency for regulating the price of medicines. Certainly, the major health insurance companies negotiate tariffs for their clients; but each company only accounts for a relatively small percentage of demand. The balance of power is therefore in favour of the pharmaceutical groups. As a result, comparative studies of drugs available on prescription and in hospitals suggest that prices are much higher in the United States than in Europe. This has long fuelled claims that, by paying more, US patients finance pharmaceutical research of benefit to the wider world. On an initial analysis, the issue is therefore the allocation of effort between nations, and not a situation in which drug owners are simply collecting rent.

But the logic of rent is now coming to the fore in behaviour that is manifestly predatory. Groups like Valeant, Turing Pharmaceuticals and Horizon Pharma engage in 'buy and raise': they buy property rights in 'old' drugs that are the only ones licensed, or still protected by a patent, or whose brand name is protected, and then raise their price, multiplying it by a factor of up to fifty. Congress and the Justice Department have taken up certain cases. Following a rise of more than 10 per cent in expenditure on medicines in the United States in 2014, the Democratic candidate made it a campaign theme. On 21 September, she tweeted: 'Price gouging like this in the specialty drug market is outrageous. Tomorrow I'll lay out a plan to take it on' – triggering a 5 per cent fall in the Nasdaq index of biotech firms. With this tweet, Hillary Clinton, the then favourite to win the 2016 presidential election, reacted to the decision by Turing Pharmaceuticals, directed by a young financier who had bought the drug Daraprim in August 2015 to increase the price of one pill from $13.50 to $750. In the following week, Nasdaq Biotech fell by nearly 20 per cent. This represented a loss of shareholder value to the tune of $100 billion.

The issue of pharmaceutical industry rents has naturally returned with the Democratic primaries for the 2020 presidential election. What is to be done? Let us cross the Atlantic. In France, Daraprim is sold under the name Malocide by Sanofi-Aventis. In November 2015, it cost €13.76 for ... twenty tablets! Four years later, its price fell even further, to €11.86.

How can a medicine be 1,000 times cheaper in France? France's Assurance Maladie is proactive in containing the rents of pharmaceutical companies. The pressure from pharmaceutical lobbies – particularly the French and foreign firms grouped in Les Entreprises du Medicament – and their infiltration of public committees of experts in France and Europe are significant.[1] But so, too, is fiscal pressure in the current context of austerity. Initial efforts were focused on encouraging the market in generic drugs. Above all, Assurance Maladie toughened its stance in its negotiations with producers and distributors.

Assurance Maladie possesses a powerful lever: it fixes the price of reimbursable products. The French market is one of the largest in the world, and the quasi-universal cover of the population by Social Security means that a pharmaceutical company has every incentive to compromise on price in order that its drugs qualify as reimbursable and eventually produces huge sales volumes.[2] For that, the company must file a request to the health authority. Next, the economic committee on health products, after a round of negotiations with the company exploiting the medicine, fixes its price on the basis of multiple parameters (medical service performed, price of products with the same therapeutic goal, potential sales volumes, lowest prices charged abroad). In fact, in the case of numerous branded drugs, France posts prices that are often below those charged by its neighbours.

This fact has not escaped Germany, where, in 2010, a raft

---

1   See the informative survey by Stéphane Horel, *Lobbytomie. Comment les lobbies empoisonnent nos vies et la démocratie* (Paris: La Découverte, 2018).

2   A company may market a product at the price it wishes if it is not covered by Social Security – and, obviously, as long as it has obtained marketing authorization.

of measures was introduced to contain the rise in the cost of medicines. These measures imposed compulsory price cuts on producers and a temporary price freeze. More profoundly, the law on the restructuring of the pharmaceutical market (AMNOG), which came into force at the start of 2011, altered the German system, which did not allow health insurance funds to negotiate prices. Pharmaceutical companies are now obliged to negotiate prices with health insurance entities for branded drugs on the basis of criteria analogous to those used in France.

A state can go even further than this by prioritizing economic and public-health imperatives. A spectacular example can be found in the French government's recourse to coercion against the Roche group on 27 August 2015. Age-related macular degeneration (AMD) is a major illness. In France alone, it affects 1 million people. Two medicines are effective in treating it, both of them developed by the Swiss giant Roche and its subsidiary Genentech. One of them, Lucentis – marketed outside the United States by another giant, Novartis – was specially developed to treat AMD. It was licensed in France at a price of around €800 per injection. Thus, in 2014 it was the top item in Assurance Maladie's expenditure, delivering hundreds of millions of euros for Roche. Avastin, an inexpensive cancer treatment, also proved highly effective against AMD. In order to protect Lucentis, Roche was opposed to the prescription of Avastin to treat AMD. The French government authorized the use of Avastin by hospitals at a cost of around €10 per injection.[1]

With no change in property rights, a change in the balance of power can therefore make it possible to cut rents – in this case in favour of the totality of patients and public health in general.

---

1   Roche initiated a legal challenge before the French Conseil d'État. The Roche–Novartis agreement was severely condemned in Italy. After a preliminary question following appeal of this decision, the Court of Justice of the EU concluded in 2018: 'The agreement between the pharmaceutical groups Roche and Novartis designed to reduce the use of Avastin in ophthalmology and to increase the use of Lucentis might constitute a restriction of competition' (Court of Justice of the European Union Press Release No 06/18).

Medicine is already one of the major segments of property held in intangibles. Can such changes be brought about in other segments without challenging property rights themselves?

The Case of Digital

Digital enterprises attract attention not only on account of scandals over the use of individual data, but also because of the scale of capitalization of some companies, which are vehicles that command sizeable rents. Initial reflection and action have mainly focused, on one hand, on taxing these enterprises, and, on the other, controlling abuse of their dominant position. The issue of taxation is a complex one.[1] For example, a proposal such as a unitary tax per user of a platform could translate into the selection of internet or mobile users by the platform, with no meaningful impact on its rents: users from whom poor advertising profits could be extracted would be excluded. For some pure players, big data – the exploitation of large databases – already creates considerable income that justifies a valuation far in excess of the investment made by the business. The French tax on the technology giants, voted through in 2019, will only bear on a small percentage of their income. The EU-wide tax will only be implemented in 2021 and its basis will be exclusively the trade in data connected with online advertising in Europe, for a pitiful yield of €1.3 billion per annum for the whole continent. Even in its broadest incarnation, including resale of data, the yield would not exceed €5 billion. It is almost as if European governments are refusing to tax the Internet giants. Similarly, they refuse to raise the economic issue of the model of payment by click in diffusing fake news, and have nothing to say when the European Commission includes in its High-Level Group on Fake News and Online Disinformation representatives of … Google, Facebook and Twitter.

---

1   See Maya Bacache et al., *Taxation and the Digital Economy: A Survey of Theoretical Models* (Paris: Paris School of Economics/Telecom Paris-Tech/ Toulouse School of Economics, 2015).

Similarly, inquiries into certain tech giants by European competition authorities have resulted in penalties certainly totalling some billions of euros; but this is ultimately a laughable amount when set against their profits (penalties whose future, moreover, is dependent on protracted court battles). In the United States, threats from the anti-trust authorities, and even from Donald Trump, are increasingly pronounced, but have not so far resulted in meaningful action.[1]

Even if the difficulties taxing the tech giants, penalizing their abuses, or even dismantling them, were overcome, the excesses of data privatization would not be at an end. In fact, the digital sector is not occupied exclusively by pure players. Big data is regarded as the new horizon of rent far beyond the Internet. Insurers count on rapidly deriving rents from it. Car manufacturers imagine themselves to be new kings of data. In the name of road safety, their future (semi-)autonomous vehicles will have to be connected to the whole environment; your car would thus become a vast hoover of data throughout your journey. The prospect of the emergence of these new competitors explains massive preventive investment in physical vehicles by a current leader in data such as Google.

Let us recall that the consecration of the property right in databases is even more recent than that of patentability. In Europe, it dates only from 11 March 1996. It is a sui generis right: it pertains to the person who takes the initiative of the database and the risk of corresponding investments. Some databases require authorization from the bodies that safeguard the use of individual data, but states do not raise any money from it. Individuals (even firms, public organizations, and so on) are also generally not paid for providing the information that feeds big data.

The current state of the law dispossesses everyone of ownership in their own information, from personal data to their 'anonymous' preoccupations as indicated by their requests on a search engine. We might therefore subscribe to a pure demand

---

1   Simultaneously, Trump has tried to prevent big tech companies from facing the small French tax by threatening to tax French wines in retaliation.

for private property rights: every individual's right to intellectual ownership of their information requires a payment by the holders of property rights in the databases.[1] We may add a second factor: free labour. A significant percentage of services on the Internet are free, but their prices should in many cases be negative. Let us take an Internet user who makes her own travel arrangements using an online reservation site and who, on her return, feeds a site with comments on the quality of the facilities. She will not enjoy lower tariffs than if she had used a physical travel agency, but will furnish her labour free of charge to the site, which for its part will extract a rent from the providers (hotels, transport, and so on). This labour also warrants its share of rental compensation.

The allocation of data flows to individuals being in practice impossible – even undesirable from the point of view of protecting private life, for example – one solution would be to introduce a system of licences. To construct or exploit a database, an organization operating physically or virtually in country X would have to acquire a licence periodically (with a rising price scale), for a tranche of terabytes of information harvested 'on' the soil of country X.[2] 'On' networks, the soil would be understood as the location of the terminal whence the information derives – for example, a mobile phone connected via an operator in country X. The state could act as a simple collector. The sums procured from these licences could even be uniformly distributed to the population. Too small to represent a basic income, what above all distinguishes this distribution is that it does not involve a social benefit: the uniformity would simply reflect the fact that almost the whole of the population in advanced countries *works* daily to feed databases.

---

1   One might also adduce the potential character as public good of databases whose possible applications are so multifarious that exclusive ownership is no guarantee of sufficient usage for society.

2   An unintended consequence would be that actors would seek to accumulate still more information in order to identify what they regard as relevant. However, this would encourage them not to retain all the information they garner on an individual (or organization).

As in the case of labour confronting capital, a reduction in the rents of property owners, even the disappearance of some of them, might materialize. To this end, new balances of forces and new tools must be fashioned and taken up to weaken propertarianism.

Conclusion
Beyond Pragmatism

On 4 August 1914, the Second International died. One by one, each of the European social-democratic parties gave its allegiance to its own country's 'sacred union'. Confronted with the reality of war, whether German or French they had to help defend the homeland and vote for war credits alongside conservatives and nationalists. The parties were joined in the 'sacred union' by trade-union organizations. In any event, what was the use of defending another way? Jean Jaurès, an ardent pacifist, was assassinated on 31 July in the rue Montmartre in Paris. And the internationalist Rosa Luxemburg languished in a German prison for much of the First World War.

Beyond its commitment to a patriotic venture, social democracy everywhere succumbed to pragmatism by abandoning the 'class struggle'. Rosa Luxemburg offered an impassioned analysis, published clandestinely a century ago in a Germany under military censorship. This text, entitled *The Crisis of Social Democracy*, is known as the Junius Pamphlet – a pseudonym borrowed from an anti-royalist English pamphleteer of the eighteenth century. In it, Luxemburg hits home:

> The cessation of the class struggle was … a deplorably one-sided affair. While capitalist oppression and exploitation, the worst enemies of the working class, remain, socialist and labor union leaders have generously delivered the working class, without a struggle, into the hands of the enemy for the duration of the war. While the ruling classes are fully armed with property and supremacy rights, the working class, [on] the advice of social democracy, has laid down its arms.[1]

During the First World War, the belligerent nations placed massive orders with the major industrialists, from Michelin and Bayer to Shell – orders for arms, tents, uniforms, and so on: everything required to organize the first great massacre of the twentieth century. Answering the German Krupp guns were the British Vickers, or the Schneider adopted by the French and US artillery. The cannon fodder were the young working and peasant classes. Having distributed flowers to the combatants at the outset, women replaced them in the factories; to increase output, they had to enter into the 'spirit of labour'. At the same time, the patriotic commitment of capitalists was ensured by the incentivizing prices agreed by states, guaranteeing the manufacturers' profit margins.

Today, even within the European Union, nation-states are in pursuit of 'competitiveness' to win or regain market shares from their 'adversaries'. Competition also operates in the financial field: the more 'credible' a state, the lower the rates agreed by markets and the higher those imposed on neighbours. These economic antagonisms are widely dramatized by big business in each country. Capitalism, which for thirty years has been free of any obligation to project a civilized image in the face of the Soviet bloc, can create a diversion. This is the manoeuvre of a capitalism that is based – from large landowners to the giants of the new economy – on the powerful protection of the property right; the manoeuvre of a capitalism that forms a genuine international: the multinationals only possess a homeland when they have an interest in so doing – for example, to benefit from a government acting as

---

1   Rosa Luxemburg, 'The Junius Pamphlet', in *Rosa Luxemburg Speaks* (New York: Pathfinder, 2011), pp. 392–3.

sales rep to flog their products and services to a dictatorship; the manoeuvre of a capitalism that incessantly threatens to outsource or relocate its activities, stimulates social and fiscal competition, and rebuffs the environmental imperative; the manoeuvre of capitalists themselves, who could not care less about borders, as they brandish the threat of tax exile and make their children citizens of the world, or rather of their world.

Confronted by such capitalists, social democracy – parties, trade unions, intellectuals – is in crisis. In the hope of gaining credibility and a semblance of modernity, in the wake of Clintonism and Blairism it has again succumbed to pragmatism throughout the 'advanced' countries. It agrees to a race to disarm labour. It even collapses in the semantic field: the protection of wage-earners becomes a rigidity, and social security contributions are characterized as burdens; the welfare state becomes a passive expense in need of proactive reform. These retreats exacerbate social democracy's inability to influence the social order.

The breeding-ground of this pragmatism is fatalism about a supposedly ineluctable decomposition of the world of labour: a world where the mass of 'less skilled' are 'unproductive'. This fatalism must be abandoned in order to supersede an impotent pragmatism.

My analysis has shown, step by step, that capitalism has entered a new phase characterized by a dual dependence: a dependence on rents procured by property rights, and on rents extracted from the labour of the 'unproductive', who perform critical support roles in our societies and economies.

This double dependence encloses capitalism in its economic and social disorders: primary inequalities, redistribution at an impasse, broken social security and public services, deflationary threats, vulnerability to unexpected shocks and inability to respond to the climate emergency. Increasing wealth-creation by broad swathes of the world of labour subjected to harmful intensification – is recognized neither financially, socially, nor even statistically. Innovation, another driver of economic growth, is progressively sterilized by real-estate rent and exclusive rights to knowledge. The neoliberal answer, which is to deepen the deregulation of goods and labour markets or even dismantle some oligopolies, is ineffective in an all-is-property economy, and can even strengthen the pressures on critical workers. Worse, capitalism unbound seems capable of surviving only by inducing the stigmatization of immigrants, the retreat of liberties, and ultimately the erosion of democracy, from the United States to Europe.

Backtracking on 'all is property' will be a protracted process. A new relationship to property in the wake of the theory of the commons might one day be established. In the here and now, states and citizens can modify the balance of forces with the owners of intangible capital in order to receive a portion of their rents. Above all, the breakup of labour is a fable; it is more than ever concentrated in a small number of organizations and confined spaces. This configuration makes possible a revival of labour, a renaissance – already visible locally – of collective movements revealing the criticality of the 'unproductive'. It holds out the prospect of new balances of power conducive to due recognition of the productivity of all. And the new sharing-out of rents that would result from this rebalancing would put capitalism back on the tracks of progress and emancipation. Social democracy, like the Democrats in the United States and Labour in the UK, has a political responsibility to grasp them to offer a genuine political alternative to the rise of authoritarian neoliberalism.

Index